MAKING DOLLARS
WITH PENNIES

HOW THE SMALL INVESTOR
CAN BEAT THE
WIZARDS ON WALL STREET

MARATHON
INTERNATIONAL
BOOK COMPANY

Madison, Indiana

MARATHON INTERNATIONAL BOOK COMPANY
PO Box 40
Madison, IN 47250-0040 U.S.A.

Telephone (812) 273-4672
Fax (812) 273-4672
E-mail: books@marathonbooks.net
Web Site: www.marathonbooks.net

Copyright ©1998 by R. Max Bowser

Publisher's Cataloging-in-Publication

Bowser, R. Max.
    Making dollars with pennies : how the small investor can beat the wizards on Wall Street / R. Max Bowser. — 1st ed.
    p. cm.
    Includes bibliographical references and index.
    Preassigned LCCN. 97-74045
    ISBN: 0-915216-98-1 (paperback)

    1. Penny stocks--Handbooks, manuals, etc.
    2. Portfolio management. I. Title.

HG4661.B69 1998   332.63'223
                                      QBI97-41065

Third Printing
Printed on acid-free paper
Printed and bound in the United States of America

DEDICATION

To Cindy, my daughter and associate, who has always been an enthusiastic supporter of my efforts.

This publication is designed to provide accurate and authoritative information in regard to the subject matter covered. It is sold with the understanding that the publisher is not engaged in rendering legal, accounting, or other professional service. If legal advice or other expert assistance is required, the services of a competent professional person should be sought.

> — *from a declaration of principles jointly adopted by a committee of the American Bar Association and a committee of publishers*

PREFACE

We hope you learn one thing from this book. That is, there is a way to make money in minipriced stocks. Use the Bowser Game Plan.

We have been studying low-priced stocks for three decades. All of that experience. All of that accumulated information. All of that has been filtered down to the Game Plan.

The advantages of the Game Plan are manifold.

1. These small-cap issues are considered risky. But, the Game Plan controls the riskiness. Through diversification. We suggest you build a portfolio of 12 to 18 or these stocks.

2. You do not have to do the research. We do. Each month in *The Bowser Report* we examine a company in great detail. We call it the Company of the Month.

3. After you buy a stock, you don't have to wonder how the company is doing. We follow up with pertinent information on each stock that we recommend.

4. When do you sell? That is the most difficult part of stock market investing. We tell you when to sell.

4a. If the stock does well, The Plan calls for you to sell half of your holdings. That way you liquidate most of your original cost. Then you track the stock's progress. If it drops back 25% from its most recent high, you sell the remainder.

4b. The stock does not do well. The company's fundamentals have deteriorated. Then, in our newsletter we tell you to sell.

5. Your portfolio can be self-financing at a certain point. The sale of stocks generates funds. These can be used to buy more stock.

6. However, you may have additional funds that you want to put into these stocks. This money can be used to increase the number of shares that you buy once you have reached your goal of 18 different issues. Or, you can average down on those stocks that you think have been unwittingly forced down in price.

Finally, there is a psychological aspect to The Bowser Game Plan. In fact, it's psychological factors that doom the efforts of many people who want to succeed in buying and selling individual stocks.

The first deadly disease is "irrational expectations." It is closely aligned with greed. It's evident when individuals put most of their money in one stock. . . . Because of the leverage that comes with these small stocks, they hope to make a quick killing.

They put $5,000 into a $2 stock. That gives them 2,500 shares. At $10 a share, their $5,000 has jumped to $25,000. Wow!

But, that $2 stock may go down to $1. They've lost half of their $5,000. . . . Putting an equal amount into 12 to 18 different issues eliminates this danger.

The second deadly disease is impatience. If they don't have a fat profit in six months, they throw up their hands in disgust. . . . Be patient. . . . Sometimes it takes two, three or four years for some of these stocks to blossom. . . . Most of the portfolios that we have operated did not do well in their first year.

One more note. It can be fun building a portfolio of minipriced stocks. You'll have your moments of anguish. And, of great delight. But, most importantly, it'll be rewarding.

— R. Max Bowser

P.S. The research that is the basis for this book was started in the 1970s. Consequently, there are many references to statistics that are almost twenty years old. However, we have retained the data that we think is still pertinent.

— R. M. B.

TABLE OF CONTENTS

"IF YOU'RE SO SMART, WHY AREN'T YOU RICH?"

This is going to be highly personal.

Normally I use the editorial "we." But not in this chapter.... I would love to use "I" all of the time. I'm so egotistical that a mirror only lasts about six months. But, a friend of mine in Columbus, Ohio, read some of my early writings and was laudatory: "If I were you, instead of using 'I' all of the time, I would use 'we.' Then people who read your stuff will think you've got a big organization."

I respect this fellow. He's smart. At least smart enough to have had a flourishing military career that culminated in a high rank and command of a large air base. Besides, I like the idea of people thinking I have a big organization.

I'm being personal, also, because I'm going to face up to the question: "If your system is so good, why not just make money in the stock market and forego the headaches and hard work needed to publish a newsletter?"

Lurking behind that question is the old maxim: "Those who can—do; those who can't—teach." . . . However, there are other justifications I could offer for spending about 60 hours a week thrashing about in this business—I'm following the admonitions of Dr. Robert Schuller, the smiling, upbeat TV evangelist. In a June 1978 telecast, he advocated: "Find someone with a problem and help him." In the same sermon, he suggested sharing your success.

Naturally, in helping you with your stock market problem and sharing my success, I expect to make money. (Of course, I'm not the only one who's thinking of you. There are many eager to help you become rich. All you have to do is buy their books that tell you how to do it.)

Too, although my approach to the market is a viable one, I don't claim that it will make you a millionaire. Apparently, a lot of people aren't interested in buying a book such as this one if you can't assure them af making a million. . . . But, how about publishing a newsletter? That must be the next thing to having your own mint.

The most comprehensive piece I've seen on market letters appeared in the September 4, 1972 *Barron's*. In it, Dana L. Thomas wrote: "A study of the advisory services quickly comes to a number of conclusions, the most sweeping of which is that it can be a pretty good way to make a buck. Anyone with a supply of graph paper and access to an offset press can go into the advisory business, assuming he doesn't have a criminal record. Making it pay usually requires some 'angle'—a new basis on which to make investment decisions. Once established, a market letter can yield excellent returns, but it has to be the most cyclical business there is. Profits fluctuate with the market averages. In an up-market, most advisory services prosper. In a down-market, they bomb."

Then, Thomas went on to observe: ". . . of the 3,811 registered advisers, only about 300 currently are publishing letters regularly, and maybe 50 of those are turning a profit on the operation."

Thus, publishing a letter doesn't seem to be the sure way to riches. . . . But, how about making a fortune in the stock market? . . . Some have.

In July 1975 the Associated Press told the story of a Southern California spinster who never earned more than $150 per month, but who had a knack for profitable investments. Minnie B. Cairns was 90 when she died in 1971 in Glendale, where she lived quietly and alone for almost 31 years. When she moved to California in 1935, all of her assets did not exceed $38,000. At the time of her death they amounted to $993,204.82.

Although Miss Cairns never revealed all of her techniques, she did reveal one rule—never buy what a brokerage salesman recommends. She felt they would tout only those stocks in which they, or their employer, had a special interest. She made her own analysis.

In April 1970 the Associated Press had another rags-to-riches story. This one was about an 84-year-old white woman in Detroit—described by a former roommate as too miserly to pay $125 for needed eye glasses. In her will she left almost $250,000 to the United Negro College Fund. Acquaintances were amazed at her wealth. Her stockbroker said that Mrs. Regina M. Peffly made the money by playing "with those little, cheap speculative stocks and she frequently bought and sold."

Nicolas Darvas, an internationally famous dancer, wrote a best-selling book, *How I Made $2,000,000 In The Stock Market.* He made his pile during the 1950s and early 1960s, during a great bull market.

Thus, maybe you can strike it rich. Or maybe I can. But, note that in each of these examples, years were required to accumulate these large sums.

Of course, you can lose money, too. That's where I come in. Let me share my bitter-sweet memories. Let's go back to the autumn of 1967.

At the time I was on active duty in the U.S. Air Force. My desk was right next to that of the section chief. (That's me. If you don't have brains, "buddy up" with the boss.) And, he was active in the stock market. He began telling me about his investments. Up until then, I knew more about the sex life of Queen Elizabeth than I did about securities. I stopped worrying about the Queen. Wall Street was my new fascination. It brought out the best in me—greed! Wow! I was impressed with the success stories swirling around me. ("Just sold Republic Corp. Made a thousand.") Suddenly, it seemed as though half of the people I knew were buying and selling shares.

"Boy! This is for me." I got out the savings passbook. Opened the strong box and dusted off the savings bonds. Added them up. Had almost $10,000. . . . I began having delightful illusions. . . . That $10,000 would soon be $20,000. Then $40,000. $60,000. In five years, at least $100,000. I could even see the obituary: "Bowser accumulated most of his wealth through clever stock market investments."

And, in addition to being greedy, I'm also systematic. I went on a week's leave in October 1967, during which I hardly ever left the apartment. Spent all my time studying the stock market. Learning the terminology. Learning how to read a stock table, Too, I tried to master the Nicolas Darvas "box method," including "the principle of the historic peak," the "On-stop Buy Order," the "power of volume," etc. . . . By the end of the week, I was ready to operate. I picked a brokerage house out of the yellow pages, and discovered in one phone call it's easy to commit thousands of dollars.

It turned out that the registered representative assigned to my account was a man with years of experience, We'll call him "Tom." . . . I told him immediately I didn't want any advice on what stocks to buy. I would choose them. And, in the six years I dealt with him, he honored that request, never offering a suggestion. . . . My first choice was 100 shares of Russ Togs. Later that day, Tom called and said, "I got your Togs.". . . Hot diggedy dog! I was in business!

Those 100 shares of Russ Togs cost $3,787.75 Eighteen days later I sold them for a $142.77 loss. During the less than two months I was in the market during 1967, I bought and sold five different stocks, each in 100-share lots. Two of the transactions were profitable. My first year in the market terminated with a $139.67 loss, But, I was determined—1968 would be a better year.

It was. For the broker. . . . Although I only had $9,245 invested, that plus what I borrowed from the brokerage firm "on margin," permitted me in 1968 to buy and sell $149,432.35 worth of stock in 105 transactions. Tom, my ever friendly and cooperative registered representative (now he's a vice president), must have done fairly well with the commissions I paid that year. At least he did better than I did. After the dust settled from all of that frantic trading, I discovered I had lost $858.16!

I made Tom work for his money. Every weekday I was calling him—two, three, four times—mostly to get quotes. And, if any man should receive an award for patience, he's the one. . . . Also, during the year, I shifted gears. I modified the Darvas method by abandoning the purchase of round lots. I used the Darvas selection criteria, but bought in odd lots, usually 10 shares at a time. The idea was that as they went up in price, I'd buy more. That's what you call "dollar-averaging up." Most of the shares I bought went down.

In January 1969 I became enamored with low-priced stocks for the first time. In fact, that month I prepared a 27-page study on the subject. At that time I defined a low-priced stock as being $10 a share or less.

Additionally, I discovered that in January 1968 there were 240 issues on the American Stock Exchange selling for $10 a share or less. I also noted that if only three of those 240 had been picked randomly, by throwing a dart, for example—those three stocks would have most likely increased to at least $5,900 by the end of 1968. So, to a guy who had been recording more losses than gains, this performance was darn impressive.

Early in 1969 I began buying shares that sold for $10 or less, with most of them being near the upper limit. The lowest was 6⅜. I was encouraged with 1969's results. I only lost $100. In fact, I thought that things were going so well I added $7,105.39 to the $9,245 I had earlier invested. I was getting ready for a big year in 1970.

Did I say a big year in 1970? . . . It started with the Dow Jones Industrial average at 809.20 and by May 26th it had plunged to 631.16 and spent the rest of the year climbing to its close on December 31: 838.92. But the damage was done in the first five months. For the first time I had the embarrassment and panic that comes with margin calls. . . . When I asked for a detailed explanation about margin operations, Tom turned me over to the office manager. The latter concluded his explanation with: "All it means is—'send money.'" And I did: $906.88.

It turned out that 1970 was my greatest deficit year. $5,103.33 went down the drain. The only benefit from this were reduced Federal and state income taxes. I would rather have paid the taxes.

By now you might think I would have been ready to chuck the whole thing. After all, there are other ways of losing money and at the same time having fun—like financing a nudist colony. But, I was obsessed with the belief it is possible to make money in stocks. I read about people who did. Furthermore, pure logic dictates that if everybody who bought stocks lost money, then eventually nobody would buy them. I was determined to find the golden key.

At the same time I knew I wanted to write about securities. Before my Air Force career, I worked on newspapers, first reporting and then editing. But, the only thing I could write about in 1970 was how to lose money. Very few people need coaching on that. . . . I decided to go to college full time. (I retired from the Air Force April 1, 1970.) I went for three years, getting degrees in accounting and business administration.

While I was going to college, I experimented with various techniques in buying and selling shares $10 or less and continued losing money—in 1971, $1,887.18; 1972, $1,074.54; 1973, $1,512.14.

Then came the dawn of a bright new day. Rather, it was in the middle of the night early in September 1974. (How dramatic can one get!). . . I woke up and while my mind wandered, awaiting the return of Morpheus, the idea struck. I was dealing with low-priced stocks, but I wasn't starting low enough. I should never buy a stock for more than $3 a share! . . . After years of posting prices daily on hundreds of stocks, I noted that when an issue climbs above three bucks, it goes on to greater heights *most* of the time.

Then I began thinking of the advantage of only buying at $3 a share or less: (1) It's impossible to have one depreciate four or five points, as had frequently happened when I bought them at $7, $8 or $9. (2) It's easier for a stock to go from $3 to $6 than for a $9 issue to double to $18. (3) It would be possible to own many different stocks even with a comparatively modest investment.

There was the need to objectively analyze a company. Previously I had relied principally on hunches. My newly-acquired accounting skills gave me the analytical tools needed to measure a company financially. The rating system was a natural development. And, finally, there was the need to reduce risk to a minimum. I didn't want any more red ink. Diversification would help to minimize the risks.

The most common mistake that investors make in buying stock at our price is that they put all of their investment money in only one or two issues. For $3,000 they can buy 1,000 shares at $3 each, and if it only goes up one point, they've made $1,000, less the brokerage fees. That makes for a beautiful dream. But, there is a downside potential. They don't always go up. If those thousand shares slip to $2 each, you lose one-third of your investment and more, because commissions will be added to the $1,000 loss. Diversification prevents you from putting all of your apples in one or two baskets.

So, with the concept of the $3 limit, the ratings and diversification, I had in essence the Bowser Plan. But now to test it. . . . In the past, I had bought stocks with my own money when trying out a new approach. This time I won't risk my own money, I told myself. I'll use a paper portfolio. Consequently, in September 1974, with a theoretical $5,000 I began buying stocks, using my new-found principles. When I discontinued the portfolio late in 1978, it had grown to over $23,000! Ironically, then, when I could have made money, I didn't actually have any of my own cash invested!

And now that I have described the Bowser Plan's painful gestation, we get back to the primary reason for writing about this embarrassingly personal experience: If the system is so good, why not make money with it and forget the drudgery of a monthiy newsletter?

Lowell Miller, in a book entitled *The Momentum-Gap Method*, makes this point: "When you start with very little money, even a 100% profit still isn't very much money. It takes time to build up capital." Which is certainly true. For, if I started with $10,000 and averaged a 20% gain a year—if you can't have that as a goal, stock ownership isn't worth the risk—and compounded the 20%, in five years I'd have $24,883 and in ten years, $61,915. This, admittedly, is a tidy sum, but hardly enough to qualify one as being rich.

In addition, as I pointed out, very few have gotten rich publishing investment newsletters. But, what they do get is recognition. I'm honest enough with myself to admit I crave it. It's a universal craving. . . . Can you imagine Roger Bannister keeping it a secret that he was the first to run the mile in less than four minutes? Or,

Neil Armstrong traipsing over the moon's surface incognito?

It has been said that deep within the worst of us, there is the desire to do good. One way that desire can be satisfied is by helping others. Fortunately, my work is rewarding in that respect. Like the unsolicited letter I received in which the writer said: "After having read through a few of your *Bowser Reports*, I feel I must subscribe to it." Or, the reader who told me he had bought $10,000 worth of minipriced stocks and had a net gain of considerable proportions.

I may not be smart and I know I'm not rich. But it has been fun despite the travail. The story has a happy ending.

SIX BIG REASONS FOR BUYING MINIPRICED STOCKS

No. 1: *Make Money*

Is there any other reason for owning stocks? None as important as this one! Our own personal portfolio of these minipriced shares has been a rewarding experience, as it has for the increasing number of others who are using the Bowser System.

No. 2: *You Can Start with Little Capital*

With only $200 to $300 you can buy your first 100 shares. Of course, we want you to diversify. You don't stop with your first 100 shares. As you save more money, you keep building your portfolio until you have at least 12 to 18 different issues. Or, maybe Aunt Tilda left you a nest egg and you can buy $3,000 or $5,000 worth immediately. And, as for the tools needed in your new investment program, a subscription to *The Bowser Report* is all you need, together with an occasional peek at *The Wall Street Journal* to check on certain Over-The-Counter stocks that you might have in your portfolio. (Most libraries have *The Journal* in their periodical reading room.)

No. 3: Minimum Effort Required

You must expect to devote some time to this investment program. Overall, the effort expended will be minimal. However, it should be a pleasurable experience. . . . The record keeping is not extensive. You might want to record each market day's prices in a loose-leaf notebook, with each issue on a separate sheet. Or, perhaps you would prefer to list all of your stocks vertically on one page followed by columns for each day's quotations. . . . The buying and selling will be accomplished with brief telephone calls to your broker. Surprisingly, you won't be selling very frequently. You will find that you'll have most of these shares for a comparatively long period of time, to allow them to develop and appreciate. The ones you hold a short period are more likely to be those that fall below a Bowser Rating of 8 and must be disposed of.

No. 4: Protection from Severe Losses

This protection comes from two features. . . . First, limiting the purchase price of each share to $3 or less, means that when you buy a hundred shares, the most that you can lose is $300 plus commissions. But, if you follow our Plan, you will have sold long before such a disastrous deterioration takes place. . . . Second, by being so widely diversified, if you do have a loss in one issue, you can recoup with the gain of one of the others.

No. 5: Little Concern with Daily Market Fluctuations

As you listen to the evening TV news and you hear that the Dow Jones Industrial Average fell, for example, 10 points, there is no need for you to panic. The mood of the market will be reflected in your portfolio. Obviously, you will do better when the bulls are happy than in a bear market. Keep in mind, though, that these are shares of companies whose earnings have "gone to pot" and now they are returning to a profitable status, or they are of young firms struggling to find their "place in the sun." When a corporation in either of these two categories reaches its goal, the market will reward its performance by bidding up the price of its shares. Here is where patience pays dividends. Concentrate on the 12 to 18 corporations, each of which you partially own, that are in your portfolio. Your primary concern is how well they are doing in sales and earnings. Don't be too overly concerned by the gyrations of the market as a whole. As long as there has been a stock market, it has fluctuated.

No. 6: Benefit of Our Research

The beautiful part of this joint venture, from your viewpoint, is that we do most of the work. We are the ones who are constantly searching for new minipriced stocks. We are the ones who spend many hours using the exclusive Bowser Ratings as part of the constant surveillance of our long list of minipriced stocks. In other words, you benefit from our research.

SELL WHEN A STOCK DOUBLES IN PRICE

Did you ever notice that when someone devises a method for playing the market, most of the emphasis is on selecting stocks and only perfunctory attention is given to selling them?

If it were possible to interview every investor across this great land of ours, we're sure that most would admit that they have lost money by selling too early, or conversely, by holding their stocks too long—seeing them climb to great heights and sinking back, sometimes to the original purchase price or less.

So, once more we are jumping into the murky waters that surround the subject of selling. . . . One thing for sure. We can't tell you in advance the perfect time to sell a particular issue—for example, when it reaches its all-time high. Only people with hindsight know the perfect time: "I should have sold it when it got up to $9."

We can give you some guidelines. We're awfully good at doing that. To wit:

From the very beginning we thought that when a minipriced stock doubled over its purchase price—that was the time to sell. Then we began having doubts.

In the August 1977 newsletter we were concerned with a stock reaching a plateau. We were worried about an issue getting stuck within a certain price range and seeming to stay there, neither going up or down; so, we reasoned, that would be a good time to sell. However, that theory proved to be invalid, for the so-called "plateau" in many cases was the pause before an upward push.

In the June 1978 issue we suggested that when a company's stock doubled, the company's situation should be analyzed and the investor then determine its potential. If the prospect for advancement in price per share is good, do not sell. If the prospect is poor, sell. But, there are two things wrong with this approach.

First of all, this presupposes that the average investor has the time and the training to make the necessary analysis. In fact, that is our job. Such advice should come with a subscription to the *Bowser Report.* (Almost anyone could acquire the necessary analytical skills with the proper application; but, one shouldn't have to become an analyst to buy and sell minipriced stocks.)

In October 1978 we conducted additional research in this matter of selling, just to recheck our theory on doubling. We went back to the October 1976 newsletter, and took a look at the 56 stocks that then appeared in "Minipriced Stocks in Buying Range." This was back far enough that it gave us a two-year perspective. Also, in October 1976, with the Dow Jones Industrial Average at 979.89, the market was high enough that any gains could not be credited to the market being so low that stocks could only go one way—up.

Of the 56 stocks that appeared in that October 1976 newsletter, 26 eventually went up 100% or more.

Seven appreciated at least 50% at some point in that two-year span. None recorded losses at the end of the 24-month period, although there were 23 that registered only minor gains.

That's the statistical aspect. Now we want to state what we think are additional reasons for parting company with these beauties after they have doubled your investment. Even though you may have fallen in love with them!

(Perhaps Will Rogers had the best slant on this entire stock market operation. His observation: "All you do is buy a stock, wait till it goes up, and then sell it. And if it don't go up, don't buy it.")

Reason No. 1: You Can Make Money
We pretended we bought each of those 56 stocks when they were first listed in the newsletter; and, when they doubled, we sold. Those that didn't double, we liquidated when their Bowser Rating went below 8, and the remainder we dumped on October 1, 1978.

So, what happened? . . . We had a 50.6% profit. And, in our book, that's not bad at all.

Reason No. 2: They Are Volatile
More and more stocks these days seem to jump around a lot in price. For instance, in commenting on a severe market drop, Michael Hirsch, Vice President of Amivest Corporation, a New York investment services

firm, was quoted in the November 16, 1978 *Wall Street Journal:* "'It's a sign of the growing volatility of the market'—that is, a growing tendency for stocks to swing up and down rapidly."

In an article on secondary stocks in the November 13, 1978 *Forbes,* the observation was made: "The rule is no longer: Buy 'em and hold 'em. Instead it is now: Buy 'em and watch 'em."

Of the 56 issues, 26 doubled during the two-year period covered in our research. At the end of the two years, 10 of the 26 were still 100% higher than at the beginning. It was not until May 1982 that the Bowser Plan was revised so that we could capitalize on those issues that continue to appreciate after they have doubled.

By May 1982, we decided the Bowser Plan had a flaw.

It's simply this: *Many times we recommend issues that eventually double and then continue to rise. Unfortunately, those who meticulously follow The Plan, promptly sell at the doubling point and can only watch with remorse when the stock they have sold continues to climb in price—if it continues to climb.*

All along we have rationalized you can take the money that comes from the sale of a stock with a 100% gain and put it into a couple of other stocks. Then they could also appreciate 100%. But, we have to admit that the number of minipriced stocks that double aren't as plentiful as fleas on a dog's back.

We have long recognized that many companies whose stock falls into the minipriced range have a rather tenuous existence. They aren't always financially the strongest of companies. After all, the market is efficient enough that these stocks are priced low for good reasons. Thus, we normally quickly suggest that a stock be sold when its Bowser Rating slips below 8. We are, then, in effect, purging the weak ones. Those left are strong because they are well managed firms that are improving their earnings. . . . Here is our experience with two of the corporations in our portfolio.

We bought 100 shares of Armatron International in Dec '79 when it was named "Automatic Radio Corporation." However, even before then it had sold most of its automobile radio business. Management in 1978 had decided there wasn't much of a future in car radios. The ASE company changed its name and began making electronic bug killers, log splitters and other products. From a loss of $1.29 a share in 1979, ART earned $1.19 a share in the first nine months of fiscal 1984.

However, we followed the Bowser Report Plan and sold our 100 shares of Armatron when they reached the doubling point at 5⅝ in April 1982. In 1983 these shares went up to 17¾.

Likewise, we sold our 100 shares of Lane Wood in February 1982 at 4⅞. We bought them in November '78 for 2⁵⁄₁₆. Traded on the OTC, LAND is in mobile homes, but increasingly is becoming involved in ladies' accessories. But Lane Wood is not doing well. Fortunately, we sold near the top.

Some time ago, Andrew A. Lanyi, a well-known NYC analyst, spotted this deficiency. He pointed out that real money could be made in those equities that make gigantic gains, like 1,000% over a period of time. And, from our conversations with Mr. Lanyi, came the idea for Gold Medal Stocks—those that we suggested be held for 200% appreciation. He did not specify that we try for a 200% bonanza. He did not suggest we call them "Gold Medal Stocks." That was our idea. And, it wasn't, frankly, a very good idea.

We have convinced ourselves we are not endowed with the ability to forecast which minipriced stocks will climb 200%, just as we can not anticipate what the market in general will do in a month, six months, a year or 10 years.

Only one of our Gold Medal Stocks performed the way it was supposed to.

Up to this point we've identified the problem. Now comes the solution. It was first suggested to us early in 1980 by Jerry Calvert of Merrill Lynch in Houston. Ira Cobleigh also suggested the solution in his book, *The Hidden Stock Market* ($19.95, Executive Planning Center, Norwalk, CT 06851). Dr. Cobleigh calls it "Operation Bait Back":

Instead of buying just 100 shares of each stock for your minipriced portfolio, buy 200 shares. When they double, sell 100 shares, hold the other 100 for further appreciation. Track the remaining 100 shares until they reach a new high, but do not sell until they recede 25% from that high. They may slip in price only 10% or 15%, for example, and then start climbing again.

As the chart on the next page shows, our revised Bowser Plan far outperforms the "old plan," for with it we only had a 25% gain. If we had been operating under our revised plan, we would have had a 70% gain, which averages out to 21% a year. That would have beat inflation, money-market funds and many other investments.

One point of caution. The chart presupposes that you would have sold at the exact point when the stock reached its highest point. Since no one can be that prescient, we deducted 20% from that 70% return, which still gives a 56% rate of appreciation, or 16.8% a year.

One other caveat: we can't guarantee that if you use our plan that you will do as well as we have outlined in the chart. After all, it depends on what stocks you buy. We usually have around 30 different issues each month in our "Minipriced Stocks In Buying Range" in our newsletter. To our knowledge, no one buys each and every one. So, just about every portfolio will be different.

Too, you might do better than we did. Many do!

COMPARISON OF THE REVISED BOWSER PLAN WITH THE OLD BOWSER PLAN
WITH STOCKS SOLD FROM THE EDITOR'S PORTFOLIO

Companies(A)	THE OLD PLAN			THE REVISED PLAN(F)				Return
	Shares	Date/Cost	Date/Sale	Shares	Cost	1st 100	2nd 100	
Aero Systems(OTC)	100	Nov 78-$257	Sep 80-$513	200	$495	Sep 80-$513	Nov 80-$917	$1,430
Basic Resources(NYSE)	100	Nov 78-$257	Dec 79-$475	200	$495	Dec 79-$475	Nov 80-$917	$1,392
Lane Wood(OTC)	100	Nov 78-$220	Oct 79-$87	200(B)	$420	Oct 79-$205		$205
Restaurant Assoc(ASE)	100	Nov 78-$251	Feb 82-$463	200(C)	$483	Feb 82-$463	Mar 82-$555	$1,018
RPS Products(ASE)	100	Nov 78-$320	May 81-$585	200	$620	May 81-$585	Jun 81-$805	$1,390
Schiller Ind(ASE)	100	Nov 78-$245	Jun 80-$162	200(B)	$470	Jun 80-$355		$355
Tech-Sym(ASE)	100	Nov 78-$270	Aug 79-$498	200	$520	Aug 79-$498	Jan 80-$1,725	$2,223
Altec Corp(ASE)	100	Nov 78-$182	Sep 79-$299	200	$355	Sep 79-$299	Nov 80-$930	$1,229
Pentron Ind(ASE)	200	Jan 79-$249	May 80-$161	200(B)	$249	May 80-$161		$161
Sterling Electron(ASE)	200	Jan 79-$304	Nov 80-$150	200(B)	$304	Nov 81-$150		$150
Tenna Corp(ASE)	200	Jan 79-$277	Mar 81-$248	200(B)	$277	Mar 81-$248		$248
TFI Companies(ASE)	100	Jan 79-$282	Jun 79-$199	200(B)	$545	Jun 79-$430		$430
Marcade Group(NYSE)	100	Jan 79-$220	Jan 82-$177	200(B)	$420	Jan 82-$390		$390
Diversified Ind(NYSE)	100	Jan 79-$239	Jun 81-$475	200	$458	Jun 81-$475	Jul 81-$507	$982
Discount Fabrics(ASE)	100	Feb 79-$307	Oct 79-$548	200	$548	Oct 79-$548	Jan 80-$855	$1,403
Frost & Sullivan(OTC)	100	Jun 79-$225	Feb 81-$112	200(B)	$420	Feb 81-$255		$255
Cognitronics(OTC)	100	Jul 79-$300	Apr 82-$300	200(B)	$570	Apr 82-$570		$570
Commodore Corp(ASE)	100	Aug 79-$287	Jul 80-$530	200	$545	Jul 80-$530	Apr 81-$1,017	$1,547
Ormond Ind(ASE) (D)	100	Nov 79-$275	May 80-$162	200(B)	$495	May 80-$355		$355
Tax Corp/America(OTC)	100	Nov 79-$275	Nov 80-$768	200	$520	Nov 80-$480	Dec 80-$740	$1,220
Armatron(ASE)	200	Dec 79-$288	Oct 80-$000	200(B)	$288	Oct 80-$000		$000
Sentry Mfg(OTC)	100	Dec 79-$287	Apr 82-$537	200(C)	$545	Apr 82-$537	Apr 82-$567	$1,104
Oiltech Inc(OTC)	100	Jul 80-$300	Jun 81-$574	200	$570	Jun 81-$574	Jul 81-$380	$954
	100	Dec 80-$312	Apr 82-$23	200(B)	$595	Apr82-$45		$45
TOTALS		$6,429	(E) $8,046		$11,207	$11,207		$19,056

NOTES: (A) Brokers' *commissions are included in all purchases and sales*. (B) All 200 shares were sold at the same time because their Bowser Rating was less than 8. (C) Because both of these stocks were sold so recently not enough time has transpired to really determine how they will develop in the future. (D) Ormand Ind. was a Gold Medal Stock and consequently was not sold until it had appreciated 200%. (E) When the Editor's Portfolio is reviewed every four months, the amount of money invested is much less than the total cost because the proceeds of sales, including capital gains, have been "plowed back" into the portfolio. (F) For purposes of this study, all of the purchases and sales in "The Revised Plan were simulated, but are realistic in that all are based on actual stock performance.

This study also points up something else—the time factor.

In the chart on the previous page, under the revised plan, the average from the time that a stock was purchased until it reached the doubling point was 17 months. However, on the average, it was only six months later that it reached its highest price. . . . It does pay to be patient!

The goal in operating any portfolio is to maximize profit. We believe that our Bowser Plan will do just that. We call it our "Revised Bowser Plan."

"There is no line of endeavor in the world where real knowledge will pay as rich or quick a monetary reward as Wall Street."

– Gerald M. Loeb

THE HANDLING OF YOUR STOCK CERTIFICATE

Okay, you've sold your stock. Now you have to get the certificate from the safety deposit box to the brokerage office. The simplest way is just to take it there in person. But, if that isn't possible, we strongly suggest you use registered mail and, at the time you register it, declare the value of the stock. To wit: if you sold 100 shares at $4, the certificate represents $400 in value. If the post office loses the envelope, they have to give you $400. . . . Be sure to keep the registration receipt!. . . . In our example, it would cost $3.60 to register the envelope with contents valued at $400. . . . Very few certificates are lost in registered mail. The investor is usually the one who misplaces them at home.

There is an alternate method. You can have the broker replace your certificate if you lose it. Check with him and decide which way you want to go.

Also, be sure to keep the confirmation slip you receive after each transaction. This is the official record of your transaction. But, keep it in a separate location from the certificate. In addition, the confirmation slip is the record you need for IRS purposes, particularly if you are audited.

Above all, don't be discouraged by these procedures. Actually, percentage-wise, very few lose their certificates.

HOW ABOUT
DISCOUNT BROKERS?

Until May 1975, brokers based their fees on a schedule set by the New York Stock Exchange. On May 1, 1975 the Securities & Exchange Commission dictated that fees be negotiated. This action has spawned many discount brokers. They do not provide the services of the full-line brokerage firms, such as research. They promise execution of orders with savings of 50% to 85%. But, those savings are only for orders involving fairly large sums of money. For an order of mini-priced stocks, they usually charge a minimum commission, which can be as high as $50 a transaction. However, some charge much less, so it is wise to shop around to get the lowest rate if you are going to use the service of a discounter.

In recent years, a new type of discount broker has appeared. It's the Internet version. And, there are many of them. Some familiar names: E*Trade and Ameritrade. . . . They feature low commissions — around $8 a trade. We even saw one that only charged $1 to trade 100 shares. . . . These are especially good for those who trade frequently, trying to capture a small gain in stock price. However, if you encounter a problem in your account, it may be difficult to contact a human being to discuss the problem. . . . For long-term investing, which is what we advocate, we suggest dealing with a broker where you have human contact.

YOU AND
YOUR BROKER

Investing in the stock market starts with a desire to do so on your part. (Isn't that profound? The rest of the paragraph is just as profound!) . . . Execution of that desire depends on the broker.

So, the first order of business is to select a broker. But, before you actually call someone in the brokerage community, let's consider criteria.

Number one is cost. What are the commission rates for buying and selling stock? Remember, you pay a commission when you buy and again when you sell. And, in your case, because of the low price of the stock, you will want to know, in particular, the minimum charge per transaction. Personally, we deal with a regional firm that charges a minimum fee of $20 for each transaction.

We should note that with the Bowser Plan, we also deal in multiple round lots. Thus, using a typical commission schedule, if we were to buy 300 shares of a stock at $1 a share, the buying fee would be $38. If it were to double to $2 and we sold, our 300 shares would bring $600, less the commission of $45.65, making our net profit on the whole deal $216.35. On the other hand, if we bought 200 shares at $1.50 each, and sold when they reached $3, the commission for buying would be $30.55 and the selling fee: $38.20. Net profit: $231.25.

With this article is a typical schedule of fees. To our knowledge, it is not the same as that of any brokerage house, and if it is, that is pure coincidence. We have merely inserted it here for familiarization purposes. In real life, the fees vary from one broker to another.

Next is the matter of execution. You may spend a month making up your mind as to what stock or stocks you are going to buy, but once you place the order, you expect it to be consummated promptly. For example, if you phone your order to your registered representative 45 minutes or more before the opening of the market in the morning, it's not being unreasonable to expect the order to be executed at the opening of the market. Your broker should have the necessary communication and related processing equipment so that your order immediately reaches the stock exchange floor for NYSE and ASE issues and the appropriate market makers for Nasdaq stocks. (Execution, normally, only takes a few minutes.)

Most firms are well equipped and have adequate facilities. However, we do recall visiting one branch office that had to phone each order long distance to the firm's home office. And, while we are an admirer of AT&T capabilities, that nevertheless throws an element of uncertainty into the execution process.

Any brokerage concern that is a member of the New York Stock Exchange will have good processing facilities, including an adequate clerical force, so that when you sell and expect cash, you receive your check in the allotted time. The same is true with your stock certificates after you make a purchase. But, if a firm is not a member of the NYSE, inquire as to their execution capability. Specifically, ask how long it would take to execute your order from the time you put down the phone to the time that it reaches the stock exchange floor. (We're assuming that the broker immediately writes up the order and promptly gets it started in the communications network.)

We have talked about costs and execution. A third factor complicating the life of the minipricer is that some firms will not accept buy orders for stocks $3 a share or less. And, even at those firms whose policy permits the buying and selling of minipriced stocks, the registered representative with whom you deal may grumble about having anything to do with issues as low-priced as these, and may even imply that there is something wrong with your sanity, or at the very least, that you are about to commit financial hari-kari.

So, let's discuss stockbrokers. . . . To begin with, "stockbroker" is a generic term. Technically, only the principals in a brokerage firm are "brokers." Everybody else selling stocks are "registered representatives" or they are sometimes called "account executives." One thing they aren't called is what they are: "salespersons." (Years ago they were called "customers' men," which smacks of chauvinism these days. Now females are involved in all phases of the brokerage business.)

The term "registered" comes from filing a form, which is mostly a character check, with the Securities & Exchange Commission. And, quite often they are required to go through a period of on-the-job training or go to a school before taking a test formulated by the New York Stock Exchange or the National Association of Securities Dealers. By the time they have gone through this procedure, they know the technical aspects of their business. Specifically, they have mastered the extensive terminology that is associated with securities trading.

They are knowledgeable order takers. As for being research specialists, which some claim to be, and some are, that is a different story and we don't have the time to go into it here. Suffice to say that they are human and they only have so many hours a day to work, and there are thousands of corporations with publicly-traded stock. Besides, in addition to selling stocks and bonds, these days many are operating financial boutiques—selling life insurance, annuities, etc.

Some of them get into a dither about minipriced stocks—due to plain ignorance. Neither they nor their firm's research department follow them. But, while they will frankly admit they don't know anything about these companies, in the next breath they will proclaim that they are extremely risky. Of course, this observation is not based on fact. Never can they cite a study to justify this sweeping indictment. We, on the other hand, have spent many years studying low-priced stocks and know that they can be profitable if the right investment techniques are employed. Those techniques are built into the Bowser Plan.

Consequently, if you have the choice of more than one broker, and assuming that the costs and execution capabilities are the same, pick the guy who will be cheerful and understanding each time you call. Fortunately, most men and women in the brokerage business are affable. Usually the bosses only select that type. Sometimes, as frequently happens in any barrel of stockbrokers, there is a rotten one.

Okay, boys and girls, we've developed the criteria for selecting a registered representative; now how do you go about finding the brokerage offices so that you can start cross-examining them? . . . Just as with a doctor, a Realtor, a plumber, etc., you may hear about them through word of mouth. A friend or an acquaintance can relate to you their experiences with a specific firm and their sales people. But, that may be only the start. Unless your friend has also been dealing in minipriced stocks, he or she may not be able to give you the specific information needed.

If the word-of-mouth route is not available to you, there is always Ma Bell at your beck and call. Walk right through the Yellow Pages until you come to "Stock & Bond Brokers" (that's the way they're listed in our book). When they answer, tell them you want to buy some stock and want to talk to a broker. Then ask the broker these questions in this order:

(1) Will you accept a buy order for 100 shares of stock at $3 a share or less? If they say "Yes," proceed to your next question. If the response is negative, call another broker.

(2) What is your minimum commission for a transaction?

(3) Are you a member of the New York Stock Exchange? (If they say "No," ask them to describe their facilities for executing orders.)

Call several firms if you can. In a metropolitan area there will be many. In some communities you will have a limited choice. Then, after you have made your calls, compare your data and make your choice. Next, the pleasant part.

This is one endeavor that can be conducted entirely over the telephone, if you so desire. Some investors prefer that their initial meeting with the broker be face-to-face and the latter may prefer that, too. Before selling someone stock, the registered representative is supposed to "know his customer." However, we had an account with a broker for almost three years before we ever saw him in person.

To open an account, you will be asked for your social security number and usually you will be required to give a banking reference. The latter is part of this "knowing your customer" routine. Also, at this point, while opening your account, emphasize that you want the stock certificate for each purchase to be mailed to you. (As soon as you get each certificate, put it in a safety deposit box. If you don't have a box, we highly recommend getting one, as they are worthwhile not only for the safekeeping of certificates but also other valuable personal documents, and the annual fee is minimal.)

MANY INVESTMENT CLUBS FOLLOW THE BOWSER PLAN

We do not know how many—precisely, that is—but, many do contact us. Obviously, our minipriced shares fit in nicely. At each monthly meeting they can collect enough money to buy at least 200 shares. In a year or so, they can have a big, diversified portfolio. . . . The females who organize clubs seem to have the most fun. For example, they frequently have amusing names, which indicates that they have fun while investing. Margaret Johnson of Billings, Montana, wrote about belonging to WHEE (Women Having Economic Experiences). We know of another group of ladies who called themselves "The Money Bags."

HOW FREQUENTLY DO YOU DEAL WITH BROKERS?

We recall speaking to an investment club. After our spiel, the most interesting question we were asked: "How often do you have transactions when you use the Bowser Plan?" . . . The questioner was a dentist, and in the back of his perceptive mind he was undoubtedly thinking that if you have a portfolio of 18 different issues, you're probably buying and selling every week. . . . It does not work out that way.

Anyone who has a minipriced portfolio will testify to that. (This is not trading. It is long-term investing.)

Or, take Maybelline—we will any day! . . . She's a part-time belly dancer and, although she built a healthy portfolio over a period of time, that doesn't mean she's spending more time with her broker than with her husband.

Nor has the time she has devoted to the portfolio prevented her from being a gourmet cook, a certified judge of roses plus being an evening student working on an advance degree. All this in addition to being a full-time nursing supervisor!

Here are the number of transactions she had in one year: January, she sold 1 stock, bought 1 stock; June, bought 3: October, sold 1, bought 4; November, bought 2; December, bought 4.

Let us get back to the point where we left you. . . . We were going to organize a vigilante committee and hang all stockbrokers. . . . We're kiddin'. . . . They're human. Just like everybody else.

Basically, what we said previously is that you have to find a brokerage firm that will accept your business in minipriced stocks. And, the number that will oblige you are numerous. After all, hundreds of thousands of shares of these mini-issues are traded daily by stock firms throughout the nation.

AGAIN—WE SUGGEST YOU KEEP THE CERTIFICATES.

Actually, there are several justifications for our emphasizing the admonition that whenever you order stock, request that the certificate be sent to you rather than be held by the broker "in street name." We advised that you keep this piece of paper in a bank safety deposit box. A lost or stolen certificate can be replaced, but that involves a certain amount of red tape and time. The delay, though, may come at an unpropitious time—just when you want to sell the shares.

In our mind, the remote possibility of your losing a certificate does not outweigh the five reasons you should keep it:

1) It will save money—not for you, but for the broker. He has to store these certificates. And, while your action alone would not justify his eliminating these special facilities, neither will he be able to blame you for having to maintain these

facilities. And, because the certificate is in your name, the corporation will mail its annual, quarterly and special reports directly to you. The broker will not have to forward these reports to you, which is a saving in clerical time.

2) By mailing the annual, quarterly and other reports directly to you, you are assured of getting this information pronto. It's important that you keep posted in a timely way on your investment. And, forwarding this information is not one of the higher priorities in any brokerage firm. (When we had our stock in street name, we recall occasionally receiving a proxy card for an annual meeting only a day or two before the event.)

3) As a shareholder you have certain responsibilities. In a theoretical sense, you and the other stockholders own the corporation. As such, you have the responsibility for keeping posted on the company's affairs and for voicing your objection or approval of what management does. But, if management doesn't readily know that you are a stockholder, and it won't if your shares are held by the broker, that in itself diminishes your authority as a shareholder.

4) If you have in your possession the certificates, when it comes time to sell, you have the complete freedom to take them to your broker of choice.

5) If your broker should suddenly cease operation, and it has your certificate, it may be a long time before you gain possession of it, even though the firm was insured by the Securities Investor Protection Corporation (SIPC). You may miss an opportunity to sell your stock advantageously.

ARE STOP LIMIT ORDERS WORTH-WHILE?

Since we advocate buying and selling at certain dollar points, one might think that a mechanism for automatically tripping action at these points would be just hunky-dory.

Of course, within the market there is a mechanism. We are speaking of a stop limit order. Such an order tells the market specialist on the American Stock Exchange, for example, that if a stock reaches a stated buying or selling price, to please execute your order at that price as soon as possible. (On the NYSE similar orders are handled differently than on the ASE.)

Suppose the last quote on a stock is exactly at 3 and you're fearful that if you order it "at the market," that by the time your order is acted upon, you might have to pay 3⅛ or 3¼. Well, you need not worry. We aren't trying to flummox you when we say that you are still within our system when you conscientiously try to buy it at 3. Besides, if it goes up to 3⅛ or 3¼ in the few minutes after you say "Buy" and the time of the execution, it probably indicates strength in that issue. We don't advise a stop limit order in this situation.

Now for a second point. Let's imagine you buy 300 shares of XYZ Corporation for $1 each. It doubles in price. Then you begin thinking about selling, but you surmise that it might go higher. It might go to $3. After all, why sell at $2 when at that price it is still within the buying range, according to the Bowser System? (The Revised Bowser Plan changes this.)

So, why not let XYZ go up to $3, but have a stop limit order at 2⅞? The 87½¢ a share difference between 2 and 2 ⅞ on 300 shares would amount to almost $262 of pure profit. . . . True . . . if it worked out that way. . . . Once it has reached $2, you know that you definitely have attained your profit goal of doubling. But, if you decide to hold, while you're waiting for it to go from 2 to 3, suppose it drops back to 1½? Then you have cooked your goose and you will have to spend more time with this issue, waiting for it to go back up to 2—if it does go back. Instead, if you had sold when it originally reached your goal of doubling, you could have taken the proceeds from the sale and gone into another stock.

Frankly, we haven't had favorable experiences with stop limit orders. When we reach a sell decision, we have it sold "at the market." It's a clean-cut operation and we then transfer our attention to other issues.

Here again, we are trying to reduce the broker's costs. Let's face it. Placing a stop limit order is time consuming, requiring almost as much paperwork as an outright buy or sale. Furthermore, your friendly neighborhood broker is charged a fee on both the New

York and American Stock Exchange trading floors for each stop limit order.

WHEN YOU CALL YOUR BROKER

No. 1: When buying or selling, before you actually tell your registered representative the action you are going to take, ask him or her to give you the latest quotation on the stock under consideration. And, you can help by giving the stock's ticker symbol, which we supply on all stocks that we recommend in our newsletter. (To activate his desk-top terminal, he punches in the ticker symbol.) . . . We insist this is important, for the stock may have climbed up out of our price range by the time you place your order. For example, we know of two minipricers who failed to do this. One paid 3¼ and the other 3⅜. Both could have avoided that if they had asked, "What is the stock doing now?"— before giving the final instructions.

No. 2: After you place your order, ask your registered representative to repeat it, so there is no misunderstanding. You don't want to have a mix-up in your order and he or she doesn't either. They will gladly repeat it and some make it a rule to always do so.

OUR RATINGS CONSIST OF . . .

Golly, we remember it well. It was the spring of 1976. We had just written the first analysis of the Bowser System. We thought it was a neat little report. At least the cover was sort of attractive.

We showed it to this young couple who had been following our work in a casual fashion. We left the report with them for a week. Frankly, we expected to be smothered with kudos when we picked it up. Instead, they said: "It was interesting; but, we don't know what the Bowser Rating is!" . . . Well, you could have knocked us over with a pigeon feather.

What difference does it make? If it works? . . . Why should we have to share our wonderful method of rating with the world? It's ours! That's like going into an automobile sales room and test driving a car, and then coming back to the garage and saying to the salesman, "That automatic shift works wonderfully well, but I couldn't buy the car until I know what the component parts are of the automatic shift."

However, actually, this simile about the automatic shift is not operational, even though at first blush it may seem that it is a pithy comparison.

It is natural to be suspicious of the unknown. Understandably, the couple wanted to know how the rating system was formulated. It was something new. There is always suspicion of something that is new. Justifiably. Not every product works out. Not every new system bears up under the intense scrutiny of time.

Then there's another school of thought. It goes something like this: "The heart of the Bowser Plan is the ratings. Why tell anyone how you make those ratings? That way there will be a certain mystery about them. Besides, if you reveal just what the mechanics are that you go through to make the ratings, why should anyone bother to subscribe to *The Bowser Report*? They can do their own analysis."

Why Are We Revealing Our Secret?

So, why are we spelling out the most intimate details of the Bowser Ratings? Why not surround them with an aura of mystery?

First of all, we believe that anyone who puts their hard-earned money (or their wickedly earned money) into the Bowser Plan, should know how it operates—in every detail. Invariably, secrecy has been more frequently used to glorify an operation, because disclosure can frequently show how pedestrian it is.

At the risk of belaboring the point, let us slip this thought into your cranium very softly. If you are determined to rate each month scores of stocks, you'd better kiss your wife good-by and rent a mountain cabin, so that you will have the necessary solitude for accomplishment of the task.

We don't think that our readers want to devote all of the time needed to duplicate what they can get in *The Bowser Report*. And, since the newsletter costs so little—for this low price we do all of the work associated with the ratings.

And, finally, by explaining in detail how the ratings are made, we hope that you will see the logic of their creation and thus have greater confidence in them and the Bowser Plan as a whole.

Why Was It Conceived?

So, now that we are going to tell all, the next logical question is: "Why was it conceived?" . . . Principally, to separate the financially strong companies from the weak ones. In the price range of $3 a share or less, there are many companies whose stock deservedly should remain in that price category. They are financially weak. They have poor managements. And, in many cases they have miserable products or services. The ratings are designed to remove the "wheat from the chaff." They were not designed to isolate the stocks that will appreciate all the way up to heaven. There you're getting into the occult. We aren't in the business of predicting the future of individual stocks, with one exception. The ratings do make it possible to avoid companies that have a miserable future.

What Are Two Characteristics of the Ratings?

And now, before we get into the nitty gritty of the method, a couple of additional thoughts as to why we are so eager to discuss the mechanics of the ratings.

It is a very subjective operation. You will note that frequently we explain something by stating that "it is based on our experience," or "we found that such and such." After all, these ratings resulted from many years of working with low-priced stocks. Hardly a day has gone by during that time that we haven't spent a portion of each 24 hours working with these lowly lovelies.

It is the embodiment of simplicity. It doesn't involve the use of computers. It doesn't require an avalanche of information about each corporation, for with many of these companies such information is not readily available. It doesn't involve a lot of complicated formulas.

How About Some Details on the Mechanics?

Obviously, we have to have a source of information. We have found Standard & Poor's publications tremendous, particularly the *Stock Guide*. It lists approximately 5,000 publicly traded companies. However, if the company we want to rate is not listed in the *Stock Guide*, we frequently write a letter, requesting the firm's annual and quarterly reports plus news releases. Cooperation has been terrific. Another good source of information when a stock is not listed in the *Stock Guide* is Standard & Poor's *Corporation Records*.

This can be found at most libraries and in most brokerage offices.

We follow and consequently rate only those issues that are listed in *The Wall Street Journal* stock tables, for the simple reason that we want the Bowser System to be useable in any part of the country. The *Journal* is truly a national publication. Conversely, if we were to have a stock only listed in a New Orleans newspaper, our subscribers in Vermont and Oregon, for example, would be severely handicapped. For once they've bought a stock, most investors like to see what is happening to it day by day.

So that you can get a complete visual picture of how we physically make these ratings—we wear an Irish walking hat, a blue jump suit and argyle socks. . . . Only kidding! We do use an accountants' 18-column pad. The one we favor is printed by Boorum & Pease, Stock Number 8818, and it is available at most stationers.

As the box on page 47 indicates, we rate 12 factors, with each factor being given a weight of one, except for current earnings, which has two. Thus, the greatest number is 13 (hardly any companies warrant a 13).

FACTOR NO. 1: Book Value

If the book value is equal to or more than the price of the stock, we consider that positive. We roughly define book value as being the difference between all of the assets of a company and all of its liabilities. If you divide that resulting figure by the number of shares of common, you get book value. (The value of preferred stock is excluded from this formula.) . . . It's surprising the number of minipriced stocks that can be bought for less than their book value. For instance, on just the first page of our May 1994 *Directory of Small Stocks*, there are 20 issues. Nine are priced below their book value. . . . Book value is Warren Buffett's favorite measure of value. In fact, many analysts focus on how stock prices compare with book value—a measure they think is more stable over time than price/earnings multiples that can zigzag wildly. . . . Charles Allmon, well-known manager of the Growth Stock Outlook Trust and a newsletter with a similar name, is on record as saying, "If I had to limit my stock selection to only one thing, I would choose book value."

FACTOR NO. 2: *Principal Business*

At times, certain categories of businesses are "hot." In the 1960s, conglomerates were popular. Whenever a single-product company began buying other companies—usually firms whose business had no affinity with that of the purchaser—the word spread that such and such a company was becoming a conglomerate. The acquiring firm's shares began skyrocketing. The concept was supposed to work because of "synergism"; but, the idea that the sum total would be greater than the results of the individual components was a delusion. The bubble began to burst when Litton Industries started faltering. This was the company that was most admired for its conglomerating. By the early 1970s, if a company was known as a conglomerate, that was the kiss of death. Now it is realized that, like every other commercial endeavor, some in this category are better than others and the prices of their shares reflect this. . . . Then Real Estate Investment Trusts had their heyday. It was almost utopia. To qualify as a REIT, they had to pay out almost all of their profits. But, when they had trouble not only finding profits but even existing as going concerns, their stock became the lowest of the lowest. (Many have recovered.) . . . At various times the clothing industry has been in vogue. Remember when double knits first came out? . . . Of course, you have the general idea. If a company is in a business that is currently popular, investors will buy those shares regardless of whether the company is making money or isn't. "Since they are in this wonderful business, they have to eventually flourish!" . . . So, any firm that is in an activity that is popular with investors, we give it an "X." We know these shares will receive an enthusiastic reception. If you are unsure whether or not a company is "hot," give it an "X" if the earnings have been up.

FACTOR NO. 3: *Sales*

Perhaps it is not surprising that many of the 10,000 or more publicly traded corporations have annual sales of products and/or services of less than $5 million. And, while $5 million or even $1 million may seem like a bunch of money, in this context it is not. Suppose we give you an example. Here's a company with annual sales of $2.5 million. Also, it's pretty doggone profitable.

It makes 10% after taxes are paid. That comes to $250,000, which is a tidy sum. But, and here's the snake in the woodpile, they have one million shares outstanding. Thus, their earnings are only 25¢ a share. A firm with such a per-share income will not go very far, unless investors are convinced that its future prospects are really great. So, we insist that a company have 12-month sales of over $5 million to rate an "X."

FACTOR NO. 4: *Highest Price Per Share in Last Two Years*

The objective of our system is to have at least each purchase double in value. The maximum that we will pay is $3 a share. So, we would like to know that at least once in the last two years it has been double its current price. If it has in that period, it's given an "X." Likewise, if our purchase price is $2 a share, we review the records for the last 24 months to see if it has been up to $4. If it has, it gets an "X". . . . Of course, it is possible that even though a company is improving its performance it has not been double its current price in the last two years. However, on the average, it has been our observation that if an issue has performed well in the past, it is most likely to repeat.

FACTOR NO. 5: *Average Daily Volume*

What should be the daily volume? The answer is purely subjective. Who knows? Nevertheless, based on our experience, we have decided that if a stock does not have at least 600 daily average trading volume, the stock is not heavily traded, and consequently is not in great demand. If 600 or more shares trade hands on the average each day during the most recent month, this indicates sufficient investor interest to warrant an "X" in this section of our ratings. If you can not find the average daily volume, give the stock an automatic "X."

THE 12 FACTORS IN THE BOWSER RATING SYSTEM

1 – Book value
2 – Principal business
3 – Sales (Annual)
4 – Highest Share Price (last two years)
5 – Average Daily Volume
6 – Dividend
7 – Ratio (Current Assets/Current Liabilities)
8 – Long-Term Debt
9 – Number of shares outstanding
10 – Earnings (last five years)
11 – Earnings (current)
12 – Sales (current)

Each factor is given a weight of one, except for Current Earnings, which is doubled. Thus, the highest possible rating is 13.

FACTOR NO. 6: Dividend

If there is a recent cash dividend, we place an "X" in this box. We aren't interested in how large the payout is. We know that very few in the minipriced range pay anything. Those that do, pay very little. In four years, the Model Portfolio only accumulated $233.25 in dividends, for an annual yield of 1% on our $5,000 investment. Nevertheless, a corporation's willingness and ability to authorize a dividend on their common stock indicates financial strength. Many companies are prevented from giving their shareholders a dividend because of covenants in their loan agreements in which the lenders say in effect, "If you have any extra money, we want you to use it in paying back the debt you owe us." On the other hand, we discount stock dividends as they merely dilute the earnings-per-share. (For those of you who haven't been hanging around brokerage offices for years, some companies will declare a dividend in stock instead of cash. Thus, if a 2% stock dividend is declared and you own 100 shares, you would be given two extra shares.)

FACTOR NO. 7: Current Ratio on the Balance Sheet

This is one of the most important facets of the rating system. This is the relationship between current assets and current liabilities. The minimum that we accept is a ratio of 1.8 to 1, which means that for every $1.80 of current assets, there are $1.00 of current liabilities. In short, the ratio must be 1.8 to 1 or higher to warrant an "X." And, the importance of this figure lies in its revelation of working capital. If a firm has $1.8 million in current assets and $1 million in current liabilities, we immediately know the ratio is 1.8 to 1; the $800,000 difference represents a healthy supply of working capital. Some of the companies that we follow will have as much as $5 of current assets for every $1 of current liabilities, while a few are at the other extreme—they have more current liabilities than current assets, which means, in effect, that they have a deficiency in working capital. When rating an insurance company or a bank, you will not find a ratio of current assets to current liabilities. Instead, use the equity per share value. To warrant an "X," this should be $3 or higher.

FACTOR NO. 8: Long-Term Debt

What can a corporation do with a tremendous amount of long-term debt? (We are not concerned with short-term debt, because that will show up in the current assets/liabilities ratio.) The answer: Excessive long-term debt is an albatross. Every year interest has to be paid on it, plus part of the principal. And, these expenditures are considered a cost of doing business, so that they are deducted before taxes and thus reduce the amount of earnings available for per-share computations. So, we say (again, strictly subjective), that if the long-term debt is more than 10% of annual sales, it is excessive and does not warrant an "X."

FACTOR NO. 9: Number of Shares Outstanding

If the ratio of available shares vs. annual sales is out of proportion, appreciation comes slowly. A good example of this is Daylin, Inc. It emerged from Chapter 11 bankruptcy proceedings late in the year 1976.

After that, the news from the company was very upbeat. Each quarterly report revealed an increase in earnings. It was in an interesting business—Handy Dandy Home Improvement Centers (the principal activity), pharmacies and apparel shops. It had excellent management. Sanford C. Sigoloff is considered an expert in reviving troubled companies. But, good as it is, sales in 1977 were "only" $292.7 million. It had 34,418,000 shares outstanding. Another company that has almost the same number of shares outstanding is Aluminum Company of America and their annual sales exceed $3 billion; Alcoa has sold for over $40 a share. Even when there was an attempt by another corporation in January 1978 to purchase Daylin, on the day of the announcement almost ¾ of a million shares were traded but the stock only moved from 2¹⁵⁄₁₆ to 3³⁄₁₆. Any other stock with a reasonable capitalization would have bounced up several points on a take-over attempt. (In March 1979, W. R. Grace & Company bought Daylin for $4.06 a share.) Meanwhile, Sanford C. Sigoloff went on to greater challenges. He is one of the small cadre of "turn-around experts." Later he used his magic with the Wickes Companies—that had gone into Chapter 11 bankruptcy proceedings. . . . The table on the next page presents what we think is a satisfactory number of shares outstanding for different annual sales figures.

ANNUAL SALES BETWEEN	SHARES OUTSTANDING
$5 to $10 million	2,000,000-2,500,000
$10 to $20 million	2,500,000-3,000,000
$20 to $40 million	3,000,000-4,000,000
$40 to $60 million	4,000,000-5,000,000
$60 to $80 million	5,000,000-6,000,000
$80 to $100 million	6,000,000-7,000,000

At $100 million and above, shares should not exceed 10% of annual sales. For example, a company with annual sales of $160 million should not have more than 16 million shares outstanding.

FACTOR NO. 10: Earnings Last Five Years

With our minipriced stocks we are concerned with growth. Consequently, we are interested in profits. In a five-year period, we are looking for a trend, and that is what warrants an "X." Of course, the trend would be obvious if, for instance, in 1980 a company earned 25¢ a share; 1981, 35¢ a share; 1982, 50¢; 1983, 67¢; and 1984, 95¢. On the other hand, if income had dipped in 1982, but resumed its upward climb in 1983 and 1984, and the current earnings are up, that would also indicate a trend, although shorter. By trend we mean at least two years.

FACTOR NO. 11: Current Earnings

In many respects, current net income is the most important aspect of our evaluation. . . . Is the latest earnings news good compared to the same period last year? If it is, an "X" is earned. And, because it is important, this "X" has a double weight. That's why, although we consider only 12 factors, it is possible to accumulate 13 points. . . . We believe current earnings are significant because:

(1) The very reason for a corporation's existence is to make a profit.

(2) Current earnings can indicate future prospects.

(3) The price of the company's stock reflects current earnings.

By "current earnings" we refer to those accumulated in the fiscal year in progress, such as are to be found in the latest quarterly, six-month or nine-month report. If there is a loss of any kind in the current earnings, no "X" is given, even if the loss is not as great as for the same period last year. This factor can be tricky to rate. Specifically, you must be on the lookout for a distortion caused by a one-time gain or loss from operations discontinued, litigation settlement and so forth. These should be eliminated when comparing the current earnings with the previous year since they are a one-time occurrence and alter the true picture of how the company is doing.

FACTOR NO. 12: *Current Sales*

Almost as crucial as current earnings are the sales during the same period of time. A decrease may indicate that the company's products or services are not being well received. However, the decrease may also be due to economic conditions over which the firm has no control. Nevertheless, a decrease in sales is not a healthy situation, as we are looking for growth in both sales and earnings. So, only an increase in current sales will result in an "X."

THROWING ALL YOUR MONEY DOWN ONE HOLE. Financial columnist Don G. Campbell received a letter from the father of a 21-year-old girl who used her life savings to buy stock in a highly-touted regional company whose shares were traded Over-The-Counter. After holding the stock for a year, she hasn't received any communications from the company. She apparently even had difficulty getting a reliable quote on its current worth.

WE'VE HEARD THIS BEFORE. This tale reminds us of the experience of an acquaintance, a secretary, who received a comparatively large sum when she quit the Federal civil service. (The money had been her contribution to a retirement fund.) She used about all of it to purchase stock in a small Dallas-based computer services firm. Right after she bought, the price of the shares started going down and she finally sold just before the outfit filed for bankruptcy. She only retrieved a fraction of her original investment. It was her first and will probably be her only venture into the market.

LEARNING A LESSON. Both of these stories are heart rending, for they need not have happened. Participation in the stock market can be a rewarding experience—even an exciting and joyful one. (We still eagerly pick up the morning paper and get a little goose pimply, anticipating what our stocks did the day before.). . . Getting back to the first girl, she obviously is a hard-working soul. Even at her young age, from baby sitting and working at a local savings and loan, she had been able to save $4,700. You can't but admire someone with that much self-discipline. . . . Chalk up another disillusioned investor in equities!

IT COULD HAVE BEEN AVOIDED. Both of these gals would not have had that shattering experience if they had enrolled in a program such as we offer. With the amount of money that they had, both could have been guided into a diversified portfolio. Both would have been told when to sell and given suggestions as to replacement shares. Both could have benefitted from the discipline of the Bowser Plan, while having the fun and thrills that can come with stock ownership.

HOW GOOD ARE THEY?

We have gone into great detail in our explanation of how we compile the ratings. Our aim was to give you a feeling of confidence in them. We didn't want you to think that when we write about a specific Bowser Rating for a corporation's stock, that we are just blowing a lot of hot air.

We do think these ratings are important. They help to make the Bowser Plan distinctive. But, it's just not sufficient that you know how they are put together. Equally important is: How effective are they in practice? But, before we start talking about evaluating them, there are a couple of other matters that we will discuss, such as our ignoring price/earnings ratios.

Why The Slavish Admiration for P/E Ratios?

Several years ago the author of the syndicated newspaper column "The Daily Investor," wrote, "When considering a stock for investment, there is really nothing more important than its price-earnings ratio." However, that sweeping endorsement for P/E ratios is not shared by everyone. (If a stock sells for $10 a share and annual earnings are $1 a share, the price/earnings ratio is 10.)

William Beaver and Dale Morse, in the July/August 1978 *Financial Analysts Journal,* explored P/E ratios and then made this weighty observation: "The price/

earnings ratio is of considerable interest, yet little is known about how it behaves over time or about the relative importance of the factors believed to influence its behavior. Differences in expected growth are commonly offered as a major explanation for differences in P/E ratios. Yet recent research raises doubt about this interpretation; past growth and analysts' forecasts appear to have little ability to explain subsequent growth."

In 1972 newspapers were talked into carrying P/E ratios in their stock tables. Yet we question their value to the individual investor, for the simple reason that a ratio results in a number and the reader of those stock tables has to know the significance of that number. This was admitted by venerable Heinz H. Biel in the January 1, 1977 *Forbes*: ". . . there is no easy formula relating the rate of growth to the P/E: 15 may be proper for one company, too high for another and unduly low for a third. That's where the analyst's judgment comes in." So, you have to be an analyst to understand them!

We don't think much of P/E ratios in general and for minipriced stocks they are about as useless as tits on a bull. These much-worshiped numbers are supposed to pinpoint real bargains. Like if all manure-hauling companies have a P/E ratio of 20 and one has only 15 . . . then the company with a P/E of 15 should be a real buy. But, maybe their wagons are decrepit, or maybe they have the wrong kind of manure, so investors are shying away from this particular manure-spreading corporation with good reason.

Then there are minipriced stocks. They're companies in some sort of difficulty or they are young companies with no track record. Most of them have what the traditional analyst would describe as "lousy P/E ratios." Indeed, frequently they are. And we know why they are. That's why we attempt to ferret out those that have a chance to survive and grow. The Bowser Ratings, as we will demonstrate, do just that.

What About The Other Formulas?

There are, of course, other measures that we could have used to determine a company's financial strength and performance, such as debt-to-equity ratio, net return on sales, etc. However, since we wanted to keep the ratings simple and easy to apply, we have restricted ourselves to the data available in Standard & Poor's *Stock Guide*, plus annual revenue figures and the latest quarterly sales and earnings. As a result, complex computations are eliminated.

How Did We Come Up With The Magic Number of 8?

Since we consider 12 factors, we could have simply said that if more than half of them are positive—in other words, if seven are favorable—we have a winner. But that would still mean that we were accepting a stock with five negative factors; and, besides, as we developed the ratings and tested them for two years, we found that eight was the key number. This doesn't mean that a stock with a BR of 7 or less will not appreciate sharply, for there can be some factors that do not show up in the statistical information, such as a merger proposal.

What Does Our Statistical Information Reveal?

To determine the effectiveness of the ratings, we asked ourselves four questions: (1) What happens to stocks that have a BR of 8 or higher and maintain that high rating for two years? (Table I). Answer: The equities listed in Table I appreciated as a group 213%. (2) What happens to issues that started the two-year period with a BR under 8 and then during the two years climbed to 8 or higher? (Table II). Answer: This group went up 196%. (3) What happens to a bunch of stocks that are 8 or higher and then in two years slip to less than 8? (Table III). Answer: They had a measly appreciation of 18%. (4) Finally, what happens when stocks that had a BR of less than 8 and never reached that rating or a higher one during the two years? (Table IV). Answer: This batch moved up 59%.

These tables, which appear on pages 61, 62 and 63, were compiled when we first evaluated the ratings and they cover the period from December 9, 1974 to December 6, 1976. All of the prices were those at the close of the market on those two dates. This study includes only minipriced stocks on the New York Stock Exchange on December 9, 1974.

It is not surprising that the group with the greatest appreciation were those that had a BR of 8 or higher during the entire two years (Table I). What is surprising is the appreciation of 59% for those stocks that were consistently below 8 during the entire period (Table IV). This is partially explained by the fact that during these two years the market as a whole as measured by the Dow Jones Industrial Average went up sharply from 571.94 to 963.26 for a gain of 68%. More understandable is the small gain chalked up in Table III, which contains those issues that started with a BR of 8 or better and then reached a lower rating; in most cases, this downgrading of the ratings resulted from lower or nonexistent current earnings and investors responded by bailing out of the stocks.

Although it is gratifying to note that collectively those equities with a BR of 8 or more did well, we have always felt that a key task of the ratings is to protect minipriced investors from the stock of companies that go bankrupt or have a precipitous decline in their finances. This is exactly what happened with Duplan Corporation that went into bankruptcy in August 1976. In December 1974 it was 1½ but by February 1976 it was 3½ at which time the BR was lowered to 6 from 9. In August 1976 when it disappeared from the stock tables it was down to 1⅞.

Our Findings

(1) Stocks with a BR of 8 or higher do consistently well.

(2) An issue with a BR less than 8 can appreciate sharply, but only because of special circumstances.

(3) The ratings give the minipriced investor an adequate warning of a company's growing financial difficulties.

(4) A BR higher than 8 does not necessarily forecast greater gains than a BR of 8.

Table I

Issue	9 Dec 74 (BR/Price)	8 Dec 76 (BR/Price)	Issue	9 Dec 74 (BR/Price)	8 Dec 76 (BR/Price)
Adams Drug	10/1⅝	10/3	Manhattan Ind	8/2½	11/7⅞
Ames Dept Store	11/2¾	10/11¾	Morse Shoe	9/2¼	12/12¾
Atlas Corp	10/1⅛	10/3⅝*	Pier 1 Imports	9/2¾	10/6⅛
Automation Ind	9/2	9/7⅝	Planning Research	8/2⅛	8/3½
Borman's Inc	8/1⅛	10/3⅝	Puritan Fashions	8/1	8/3
CLS Corp of Amer	10/2¾	8/4½	Rexham Corp	10/2⅛	10/9⅞
Cluett Peabody	8/2⅞	10/9½	Rite Aid	9/2⅞	12/17
Computer Sciences	8/2⅛	10/7⅛	Safeguard Ind	9/1¾	10/4⅞
Elixir Ind	9/2¾	10/7⅝	Sanders Associates	8/2½	10/8⅞
EMI Ltd	8/1½	8/3⅝	Sav-A-Stop	8/1⅞	8/3½
GCA Corp	***?	9/7⅛	Savin Business Mach	10/2¼	12/17 ⅜
Helene Curtis Ind	11/2¼	10/5⅜	Simmonds Precision	10/2½	10/6
Ipco Hospital	9/2	9/5¼	Sterling Precision	9/2¼	10/5¾
HMW Ind	9/2¼	8/3¼	Suave Shoe	8/1¼	8/4¾
Keene Corp	10/3	10/9⅞	Union Corp	8/2¾	8/5⅞
LFE Corp	10/2¾	9/4⅜	Whittaker Corp	9/1⅛	9/6
Loral Corp	10/2⅛	12/4⅛			

*In November 1976 shareholders approved a l-for-5 reverse split. On December 8, 1976, Atlas had a Bowser Rating of 10 and a price of 18⅛, which is equivalent to 3⅝ if there had *not* been a reverse split. ("BR" means "Bowser Rating.")

Table II

Issue	9 Dec 74 (BR/Price)	8 Dec 76 (BR/Price)
Adams Millis	7/1¾	10/4
A. J. Ind*	5/1⅜	9/4⅜
Applied Magnetics	7/⅞	8/3¾
Arctic Enterprises	5/1¼	10/4⅛
Berkey Photo	7/1⅞	9/3⅞
Cadence Ind	7/1¼	8/3⅜
Caesar's World	6/2½	8/3⅞
CCI Corp	5/¾	8/4⅜
Chris Craft Ind	7/2	9/6
Coleco Ind	5/1¼	9/5

Issue	9 Dec 74 (BR/Price)	8 Dec 76 (BR/Price)
Donaldson Lufkin	6/2	9/3⅞
Levitz Furniture	6/1¾	9/6
MacDonald (E. F.)	6/1⅛	9/6
McCrory Corp	7/1¾	**
MEI Corp	7/1¼	8/4½
Mohawk Data Svcs.	7/1⅛	8/5⅞
Phillips Ind	7/2¼	10/7⅞
Venice Ind	7/1⅝	1⅓/3¾
Wolverine World Wide	7/1¾	10/4⅝
Webb (Del. E.) Corp	6/2¼	8/9

* Has since merged.

** No longer traded

Table III

Issue	9 Dec 74 (BR/Price)	8 Dec 76 (BR/Price)
Diversified Ind	8/1⅝	6/1⅛
Duplan Corp	9/1½	*

Issue	9 Dec 74 (BR/Price)	8 Dec 76 (BR/Price)
Electronic Mem&Mag	8/1	7/3⅜
National Tea Co	8/2¾	5/3⅝

* In August 1976 Duplan Corporation went into bankruptcy.

Table IV

Issue	9 Dec 74 (BR/Price)	8 Dec 76 (BR/Price)	Issue	9 Dec 74 (BR/Price)	8 Dec 76 (BR/Price)
Aileen	7/1½	6/3⅛	Horizon Corp	5/1½	5/2
Allied Supermarket	6/2⅛	5/2¾	Lehigh Valley Ind	5/½	5/1
Amrep Corp	5/1½	4/1¾	Lionel Corp	7/1	7/3
Apeco Inc.	5/ 13/16	5/1½	Morse Electro Prod	7/1¼	*
Arlen Realty & Dev	6/1½	5/2⅝	Penn Central Co	5/1⅛	**
Bobbie Brooks	7/1	6/3¼	Redman Ind	5/1¼	6/3⅜
Carling O'Keefe	7/1⅜	7/3	SCA Services	6/2	7/2½
Chock Full O'Nuts	7/2½	6/2¼	Sonesta Int'l ****	7/2⅛	7/3⅝
Cordura Corp	6/1	6/2¼	Telex Corp	5/2¼	7/2⅝
Electronic Assoc	7/1⅛	5/2⅛	United Park City Mine	5/1⅝	4/2⅞
Grolier Inc ***	6/1¼	6/1¼			

* Delisted in August 1976 by the NYSE for failing to meet certain financial criteria for continued listing.
** Suspended by NYSE effective August 2, 1976.
*** Delisted by NYSE in 1977 for failure to meet listing requirements.
**** In August 1978 company purchased most of its shares and thus no longer met NYSE listing requirements.

EDITOR'S NOTE: While the above tables may seem like ancient history, they were pertinent at the time we were evaluating our rating system.

WANNABE OSTRACIZED? BUY MINIPRICED STOCKS

Here's hoping we don't come across as a whiner with the words we're about to write. . . . But, admittedly, we're upset. About minipriced stocks.

They're being discriminated against.

You've heard of political correctness? Of course you have. It's rampant in many of our major universities. If you don't have politically correct thoughts, your viewpoint isn't tolerated.

Mike Royko, the famous *Chicago Tribune* columnist, wrote about political correctness: "Universities are supposed to be symbols of open thought and discussion. But, you can find more openness and enlightenment in your neighborhood saloon."

Likewise, there is such a thing as economic correctness in the securities industry. In the centers of influence in the industry, there is no tolerance for stocks $5 a share or less. $3 or less? Forget about 'em.

Even the financial press is prejudiced and gladly distributes misinformation about them. For example, in *USA Today*, Carey Newton of Bowling Green, KY, innocently asked, "How could I find out more about penny stocks?"

The Kentuckian was told by reporter Chris Wloszczyna: "Penny stocks trade for $5 a share or less on a variety of local exchanges. [That implies they aren't on the NYSE, Amex or Nasdaq.] They can be bought through a broker, like any other stock, although major brokers seldom recommend them. . . . Think long and hard before buying penny stocks. Prices are hard to find because the stocks trade so rarely."

Bowser Report subscriber Clarence Reinders, Marshfield, WI sent us a column written by nationally-syndicated William A. Doyle. In the column, Mr. Doyle wrote: "Forget about penny stocks, which are defined as those trading below $5 per share. . . . There has been a tremendous amount of fraud in penny stocks. Even when everything is on the up and up, penny stocks generally are far more risky than higher-priced issues."

Mr. Reinders has done well with our low-priced babies. In fact, he was featured on our front page in January 1993. Clarence, in commenting on Mr. Doyle's column, wrote, "How do you counter this prejudice against your minipriced stocks?"

The Wall Street Journal has noted its conception of "penny stocks": "These are shares of stock in small companies that trade over the counter. They are called 'penny' stocks because their share price may be mere pennies; such stocks usually sell for less than $5 a share. But, penny stocks are rarely a bargain at any price, the experts say. They are highly speculative, thinly-traded and have huge hidden markups. . . ."

As for the industry itself, anyone who has tried to buy a $2 stock at a major wire house, such as Merrill Lynch, Dean Witter, etc., know they are subjected to harassment.

Ironically, though, these same small companies are being heralded as the ones creating so many new jobs. Yet, as far as Wall Street is concerned, most of these companies don't exist.

A couple of years ago, the editor of *The Bowser Report* was the speaker at a dinner meeting of a New York City brokers association. As part of the presentation, the Bowser Game Plan was outlined.

After the speech, a group of brokers from major brokerage houses told us that if they sold 12 to 18 of our stocks to their clients, they would be fired. However, they conceded that our approach works.

The success of our plan was demonstrated within the ranks of the "enemy"—in the Pasadena, CA office of Shearson Lehman Brothers.

Subscriber Thad Williams, a Shearson Lehman financial consultant, won the annual office stockpicking contest. It's called P.O.O.P. (Pasadena Office Outstanding Picks).

Thad captured first place, using ten of our selections. During the year, he had a gain of 46% and beat Shearson's Uncommon Values Unit Trust. This is an investment vehicle into which Shearson's researchers put what they consider their ten best stocks. The Trust was up 35%.

Even on the cocktail circuit and over the water cooler, low-priced stocks are disparaged. George Crissman, San Diego, CA, experienced that prejudice. George wrote:

"Thank you for an excellent first year of investing! When I first started, I was pretty much the object of ridicule, because I wasn't buying the 'big name' stocks that 'you are SUPPOSED to own,' as far as my acquaintances were concerned.

"'Oak Industries? A buck fifty a share?' they sniffed. 'Nah—you'll be lucky to get your money back on THAT mangy issue.'

"Twelve months later, OAK is trading at $25 per share . . . and my advice and opinions on investing are highly prized by those I know. My advice hasn't changed over the months either: subscribe to *The Bowser Report*, follow the Plan and you'll do OK." [Oak was as high as 29 after a reverse split, but it's now around 16.]

Of course, the high-priced stocks aren't always the big winners as promoted. For example, even though *The Wall Street Journal* does not think much of penny stocks, the paper admitted last month that "the biggest stocks aren't always a safe bet."

MANAGING YOUR MINIPRICED PORTFOLIO

BOWSER'S GAME PLAN

1 - Select from our recommended stocks on pages 3 and 4 of the Newsletter.

2 - Buy at least 200 shares.

3 - Diversify. Keep buying until you have a portfolio of 12 to 18 issues,

4 - When a stock doubles, sell half of your holding. Track the remainder. When it drops 25% from its most recent high, sell.

5 - If a stock deteriorates and we say "sell" — you sell.

6 - Selling will be your most important function. You do not make money holding "dogs" — hoping some day they will recuperate.

7 - Be willing to spend some time on your portfolio.

POLICY STATEMENT

We think it's important that right along with you we buy and sell stocks. The same ones we recommend. Otherwise it would be like a teaching pro at your local club or links having never played golf. He or she just tells others how to play.

For over 20 years we've been personally buying minipriced issues. However, we decided to start a portfolio that was specifically based on some techniques we have fine tuned. These are techniques necessitated after low-priced stocks fell out of favor in 1983. We were spoiled in the late 1970s and early 1980s. Then, it seemed, every stock we picked usually went up.

A model portfolio, we decided, wouldn't do. It is far different to actually own stocks than to make believe you are selling and buying issues. For example, the executed price is quite often different than the price that comes from retroactively looking at a stock table. Also, when your own money is on the line, YOU have an emotional involvement.

To avoid a conflict of interest, we never buy or sell an issue until one week after the newsletter suggesting such an action has reached our subscribers. (We have the brokerage confirmations validating our buy/sales and timing.)

Furthermore, we determined not to print the Portfolio in the newsletter. Then the stocks in it would be the focus of attention. We don't buy every issue in Minipriced Stocks in Buying Range. Just as you don't. And, while we spend many hours trying to pick the Company of the Month, we have no greater insight as to actually what will happen to it in the future than you do after you see the results of our research. We don't want to influence your selections.

Frankly, we have used the "Editor's Personal Portfolio" for promotional purposes. If you are a recent subscriber, you have seen it. In addition, we have offered to mail it to those readers who have not seen a copy. It will be automatically distributed upon renewal. . . . We publish a new summary of our purchases and sales every few months. The most recent summary shows that since it was initiated in 1986, there has been an annualized gain of 24.2%. Following is the beginning of a series on the techniques used to get that very substantial gain.

— R. Max Bowser

NOT EVERYONE LIKES
DIVERSIFICATION

Aren't mistakes wonderful. . . .They are an important part of the learning process. Some of man's great discoveries came from mistakes. Nylon was one of DuPont's great "mistakes."

All of this was stimulated by a letter from David A. Madsen, of Akron, Ohio. He wrote:

"I'm an individual investor who's learned a lot over the last 10 years from *The Bowser Report*, my own investment mistakes and personal research. I think your newsletter is invaluable to the individual investor. It's the only newsletter I've stayed with during that entire period, after sampling many others. You've proven that minipriced stock investing works and you've made me a believer in this segment of the market."

Thanks for the plug, Dave. . . . But, when the Great Tabulator in the Sky is making a compilation of those who benefited from mistakes, we'll be at the head of the list. As we indicate in the Policy Statement on the other page, we've had to change our investment techniques, due to past errors.

Because of those changes, beginning in 1986 we were able to take $4,454.15 and turn it into $16,051.04 in four years.

However, there is one technique we haven't changed. We still believe in diversification, as do most successful financial planners. This is a basic tenet. Not only as to the number of stocks an individual owns, but also as to the different types of investments. But, everyone is not a believer.

No Diversification for Dick

Dick Davis was a Miami-based broker with Drexel Burnham and initiated an outstanding market letter bearing his name. In the May 9, '83 *Forbes*, Dick said:

"In selecting a portfolio, lean toward concentration instead of diversification. By spreading out all over the place you reduce your risk, but also limit your gains. Own enough of a stock so that if it is a big winner it will mean something in dollars and cents."

True. True. Up to a point. We've all heard that if you'd put $1,000 in IBM 50 years ago, you'd be a millionaire now. But, how many IBMs, Xeroxes, etc. are there? Not many. You might spend the rest of your life trying to find one of these super stocks. Especially in our cozy little universe.

Of the 417 issues we've recommended since 1977, only 11, as of the latest tabulation, had gains of over 1,000%. Yet, the great majority of them had smaller but still substantial gains at one point after we picked them. A gain of 100% is pretty substantial in our book.

Dealing with Risk

Dick Davis did concede that diversification reduces your risk. And, regardless of a stock's price, there is risk. But, with cheapies—such as ours—you might as well be a matador riding into the bullring. Let us illustrate.

One of our more sanguine subscribers called and wanted to know why Marcade Group had slipped in price. Of course, we would like to know, too.

But, we are concerned about that phone conversation. It bothers us that he said he bought 10,000 shares of MAR after we had such a ringing endorsement of the company as part of a June '89 interview with President Charles Ramat.

Marcade in June '89 was 1⅞. It later slipped to 1⅛ or so. That means his $18,750 investment is now worth $11,250, for a paper loss of $7,500 plus commissions. . . . While that might not be much money to Donald Trump, to us that's a lot of wampum.

Worry, Worry, Worry

We doubt this gentleman has a portfolio of 18 minipriced stocks, each in 10,000-share lots. The worried tone of his voice leads us to believe he put most of his eggs in a basket marked "Marcade."

A holding like that can create a great deal of anguish. Those who argue against diversification don't mention that factor. (We also bought Marcade at 1⅞, but only 400 shares.)

Mutual Fund Diversification

Ironically, one frequently cited reason for buying a mutual fund is because of the great diversification you get. Thus, doesn't it make sense that as an individual you should also diversify?

THE EDITOR'S PERSONAL PORTFOLIO

With minipriced stocks our Personal Portfolio makes the point that a series of little gains can add up to a significant amount over a period of time.... Even though the Portfolio was started in '86, the first summary was not published until 9/6/88. Surplus cash did not enter the calculations until 6/6/89, when it became a significant factor. *A total of $4,454.15 of our own money has been invested in the Portfolio.*

Following is a condensation of each of the published summaries:

9/6/88	
MARKET VALUE 11 STOCKS	$7,361.25
PREVIOUS GAINS	741.90
DIVIDENDS	103.78
TOTAL VALUE	$8,206.93

12/8/89	
MARKET VALUE 12 STOCKS	$7,669.50
PREVIOUS GAINS	4,014.94
SURPLUS CASH	3,305.09
DIVIDENDS	245.85
TOTAL VALUE	$15,235.38

7/12/91	
MARKET VALUE 13 STOCKS	$9,558.75
PREVIOUS GAIN	10,018.21
DIVIDENDS	698.62
TOTAL VALUE	$20,275.58

8/17/92	
MARKET VALUE 12 STOCKS	$14,581.29
PREVIOUS GAINS	13,774.56
DIVIDENDS	965.21
TOTAL VALUE	$29,324.06

2/2/94	
MARKET VALUE 17 STOCKS	$15,806.25
PREVIOUS GAINS	22,422.19
DIVIDENDS	1,352.96
TOTAL VALUE	$39,581.40

REVERSE SPLITS

As with most of your subscribers (read disciples), I too have won some and lost some in following the Bowser Plan. My current dilemma focuses on how to set a price gain goal on stocks having had a reverse split.

A by-guess and by-gosh, seat-of-the pants, totally arbitrary number may be just as good as the next fellow's guess. However, I am one who enjoys having at least a little order, reason and realism underlying my money moves. . . . What guidance can you offer?

—Don Fitzpatrick, Orlando, FL

Editor: With reference to determining a selling point on a reverse split, we simply consider the amount of money invested in the stock and then determine what the price would have to be for us to double that investment. At that point, we kick in our Selling Plan—sell half the holdings and track the remainder to see if it drops below 25% of the high and then sell the remainder.

DIVERSIFICATION IS A NECESSITY

Do you like to play with words and phrases?

Take the simple little word "come." Our dictionary says it has 62 different meanings.

Or take the phrase "long term."

For the desperado scheduled to die in the electric chair in one week, long term is less than seven days. For the fellow who is 95, tomorrow is long term. For the 21-year-old, long term is 30 years or more.

When it comes to interpreting this phrase, with our minipricers all of the above applies. . . . Some expect immediate results. . . . Others apparently make a lifetime commitment.

Soggy Ice Cream Bar

We talked to a delightful Minneapolis lady who had bought about $1,500 worth of Chipwich right after it was our Company of the Month. After she acquired the stock, she bought a Chipwich ice cream bar. She thought it was "soggy." However, she said that might have been because the vendor had it on hand for awhile.

Nevertheless, two months after she picked up the stock, she sold it for a loss. None of this long term stuff for her. Bing! Bang! If it does not go up right away, sell it.

But, it does pay to stay with a good stock. . . . We need look no further than Cabot Medical Corp. for an illustration of how a stock can simmer for years and then the market suddenly recognizes it as a great one. Later, it went up over 205% in one month.

We first selected Cabot in Jun '86 when it was 2. In the next four years it fluctuated between ⅞ and 3¼. But, what is important is that in all of that time there was no reason to sell. The company had some down quarters, but was always profitable. The Bowser Rating never slipped below 8.

Little Immediate Gratification

Very seldom do we select a stock and it promptly climbs to high heaven. Most sit and marinate for months and months before beginning to rise. Some examples: Artistic Greetings, CSM Systems, Halsey Drug, Hospital Staffing, RCM Technologies, Hycor Biomedical and Utah Medical.

Our subscribers who've made big money with Telefonos de Mexico are those who bought for peanuts several years ago and patiently held on.

Nevertheless, there are reasons to sell. Most of the time it's because the company's performance is deteriorating. Failing to sell a deteriorating stock not only means a loss of money, but also considerable agony.

We were reminded of this last month when we received a copy of a letter that C. R. Parrott of

Darlington, SC had sent to Charles R. McConnell, president of TVI Corporation. Mr. Parrott bought some TVIE shares shortly after we recommended the company in Feb '84 at 1¹³⁄₁₆. The issue did appreciate a little—to 2⅛. In recent years it has been headed south. (Now TVI Corp. is 1¢ bid in the Pink Sheets.)

Frustration, Frustration, Frustration

To put it mildly, Mr. Parrott is frustrated that President McConnell stopped corresponding with him. The following gives the flavor of C. R.'s letter. He was trying to figure out why McConnell had not answered his Jun '87 letter: "Did you kick the bucket? That thought flittered through my mind but I dismissed it, saying that the world could not be that lucky."

Admittedly we were slow in dumping TVIE. Not until Oct '88 did we recommend that TVI Corporation be sold. In Oct '88, the price of this military related stock was ³⁄₁₆. Selling hardly raised enough for brokerage fees.

But, most importantly, C. R. would not have been abusing his ulcers for the last 20 months (or in the future) agonizing over the stock. Talk about Chinese water torture!

Holding on Forever

People will call up and ask about stocks we suggested be sold eight or nine years ago. Usually by now they have sunk into the Pink Sheets. Our callers are almost begging for just a little morsel of information. "Could you please give me their phone number?"

Just as we were writing this, the following note was put on our desk from Bob Szabo, Liverpool, NY: "Could I please have an update for American Sports Advisors Inc. Recently there was a 1-for-10 reverse split. New management, new direction. Any information would be appreciated."

In our Jun '86 edition we said unequivocally that American Sports should be sold. The price then was 31¢. Never was a winner. Selected in Jan '82 with a price of 1³⁄₁₆. Later in 1983's bull market for low-priced stocks, this issue climbed to around 2½.

We looked it up in the Pink Sheets and found only two market makers willing to deal. They'd give you 75¢ if you wanted to sell. Or, if you wanted to buy American Sports, you'd have to pay $2.75 a share. We have to assume Bob never sold in 1986.

Importance of Selling

The salient point is that after we recommend they be sold, only about one out of 20 ever comes back. We don't just casually suggest your selling. When we make those decisions we are very much convinced they have had their day in the sun. And, remember, in this game, you are playing the odds. We do not think 1-in-20 is good.

We equate building a portfolio of minipriced issues to growing flowers in your front lawn. If you do not dig up the dying plants and instead just hope they revive, you will eventually have a flower bed of mostly dead plants. And, instead of telling people about your beautiful plants, you will be moaning about your awful flower bed and how you do so poorly as a horticulturist.

Selling Distressed Goods

Since we initiated "The Editor's Personal Portfolio" in 1986, we have sold three stocks because they were placed in Catch-22. Here is what happened:

COMPANY	SELLING PRICE	LOSS	PROCEEDS	PRICE 2/15/97
HELM RESOURCES	3/8	$109.65	$136.18	5/8
MESA OFFSHORE	1	$193.79	$177.99	N/A
CARDINAL IND	5/8	$104.91	$115.09	0
			$429.26	

We have the satisfaction of knowing that two of these disposed stocks are lower than when we sold. The other (Helm) is up only ¼. In addition, we have stopped thinking or worrying about these three.

And, even if they do stage a miraculous turnaround, we will have no regrets about selling them. That would merely be crying over spilt milk. As it is, in this business, there are entirely too many decisions based on hindsight. "Oh, I wish I had bought that." Or, "I wish I hadn't sold that."

Too, we have to keep in mind that when we sold Helm, Mesa Offshore and Cardinal, we received $429.26 in proceeds. With this money we were able to buy another issue—maybe a better performing one.

Selling the Big Gainers

Now let's change gears. . . . Up to now we've been discussing distressed merchandise. A happier predicament comes up when you have a big gain in one of your stocks. Fortunately, quite a few of our picks have appreciated substantially.

When a stock starts going down the chute, we make the selling decision simple. Likewise, we have simplified the selling process when one of our babies escalates.

For a long time we have advocated selling half of your holdings when the issue doubles in price. Thus you liquidate your cost. After that you track the stock and sell when it drops back 25% from its most recent high. Let's illustrate with Halsey Drug.

Saying Goodbye to Halsey

We bought 200 shares of HDG at 2⅜ for $499.57 (including commission) on 3/13/87. On 4/18/89, after it had doubled, we sold 100 @ 5³⁄₁₆, receiving $498.73.

Halsey continued to slowly move up. On 4/25/89 it was 6⅜; 6½ on 5/15/89 and on 5/25/89 it closed at 7¼, which turned out to be the highest it has ever reached. At the time we were saying that an issue should be disposed of if it drops back 20% from its most recent high. (Now we are using 25%.)

Twenty percent of 7¼ is 5.80. On 6/21/89 we sold our remaining shares at 6. We had 110 shares, 10 of which had been given to us as a stock dividend, netting us $635.05. Add this to the proceeds from the first sale and you have a total of $1,133.78 for a gain of $634.21.

Since we got rid of Halsey, it has languished between 4 and 5 most of the time. Whether it will ever exceed its high of 7¼ we don't know. Some stocks reach a plateau and just stay there. Maybe Halsey is destined to be a $5 stock.

Greed can make the selling decision difficult. When an equity is on an upward curve, there is the natural inclination to think, "I'd better not sell. It'll go higher."

TURKEYS AS MANAGERS

Minipriced stocks are fragile entities. Invariably they are small companies with limited assets. One or two mistakes in employing those assets and the companies have had it. Most of the time those mistakes are the result of poor management.

In fact, corporations in this price category have difficulty in attracting top-notch managers. Sadly, from the perks granted them to the out-of-line salaries and bonuses that cooperative boards of directors shower on them—you'd think they were great industrial leaders rather than the turkeys they really are.

Thank God! There are some excellent managers in this group. But, you don't know who they are until the market begins recognizing their competence and the stock price begins climbing. That is why you need to diversify. So that your net will catch one of these pearls.

THE VIRTUE OF SELLING

There are more low-priced stocks than high-priced ones. A close look at the NYSE, ASE and Nasdaq stock tables will verify that.

It is also true that low-priced issues can go to pot more quickly than their higher-priced brethren. Yet, despite this unattractive characteristic, money can be made with the tiny ones. And, the beauty of it all is that less capital is required.

It's all in how you play the game.

To be successful, you have to realize that if you buy, say, 10 stocks—six or seven will depreciate. But, the three or four winners will more than compensate for the losers.

Here are the two biggest errors that minipriced stock players make:

Mistake No. 1: Putting all their money into one stock.

It's great if you happen to get a winner. Put $10,000 in a $2 stock. It goes to $5. You've racked up a gain of $15,000. But what if instead it goes down to $1? Or, even becomes worthless?

To protect yourself, you must diversify—as we have advocated so many times. Spread your investment among at least 12 companies.

Mistake No. 2: Failing to sell laggards.

Many investors seem almost fatalistically inclined to stick with losers. Even after the company reports quarter after quarter of losses. Or, even after the price of the stock has dropped 80% below the purchase price. They still hang on, hoping for a turnaround.

Sell at the early signs of deterioration and put the money into something more promising. (We help you by recommending when an inferior stock should be sold.)

What we have written so far is like the defensive part of a football team's strategy. . . . Now we turn our attention to the offensive.

What do you do when you have a big gainer?

As we pointed out previously, when a stock doubles, sell half of your holdings. That liquidates your cost. With the remaining half, follow it closely. When it drops 25% from its most recent high, sell the remainder.

Some criticize this as being too mechanical. That instead, you should reanalyze a company when the stock reaches a new high and determine if it is going higher or if that is the highest it will go.

Frankly, that's a lot of hogwash. That's calling for greater analytical powers than we have. It also calls for the ability to predict the future—an ability only belonging to the Good Lord and Joe Granville.

Our mechanical approach to selling the high risers has worked like a charm.

Earlier we related our experience with Halsey Drug. We bought 200 shares in March '87 for $499.54 (including commissions). We held them until Jun '89—or just a little over two years. The first 100 shares were sold at 5 ³⁄₁₆; the second at 6.

Then there's our delightful experience with Cabot Medical Corporation.

We bought 600 shares in Aug/Sep '86 for an average price of $1.38. They cost us $826.80 with the broker's fee. In May/Aug '90 we sold the 600 for $4,831.56. Thus, we had a net gain of $4,004.76.

In May the first 200 were sold for $932.90. This covered our original cost. In August the final 400 went for $3,898.66.

Cabot is a medical device company that is well managed, and has since been acquired by another company. And, since it has excellent leadership, it put itself in the position to capitalize on laparoscopy instrumentation, which results in less invasive surgery.

A laparoscope is a medical telescope that projects a patient's innards on a TV screen. With slim surgical instruments, the surgeon can work through a half-inch incision in the navel and not disturb slow-healing stomach muscles.

In 1986, the stock market suddenly realized that the companies making this equipment were about to have a bonanza.

CBOT shares began climbing to what was, for it, dizzying heights.

During that month it shot up so fast it passed our doubling point, which was 2¾. We sold our first shares at 4¹³⁄₁₆ on May 24. . . . The stock continued to soar, reaching its closing high of 13¼ on July 26.

After that, the price began slipping. We knew that if it got down to 9¹⁵⁄₁₆ , we would sell, because that would be 25% below the high of 13¼. On Aug. 7 we sold our remaining 400 shares at 9⅞. (Seldom can you hit these selling points precisely.)

When Cabot was well over 13, someone called and asked, "Should we sell now?" We replied, "Stick with the selling plan."

Although they didn't say anything, we can well imagine them thinking, "He says don't sell now but if it goes down 25%, sell. That doesn't make sense."

Why didn't we sell Cabot when it was 13¼?

As we look back, we agree that it would have been wiser to sell at 13¼. But, we aren't making that decision today. We didn't know that 13¼ was going to be its high.

We knew that the driving force behind this stock's climb was not its increase in earnings and revenues. For years it was just another medical device company specializing in gynecology instrumentation. Suddenly it became a concept stock because of the laparoscopy instrumentation. It could have continued to skyrocket.

With concept stocks, investors get great visions of wealth and growth. We know of a little company with a telephone switching device that went from less than 3 to over 100. And then, there was Xerox. It was initially a concept stock when it first introduced the plain-paper copier.

When CBOT reached 10, we had to make a decision. But, it kept climbing to 11⅛. Why not sell at that point? Then it got up to 12¼; our 400 shares would have been worth almost $5,000. Nevertheless, we resisted and stuck to the plan.

The down market may not have been the only reason Cabot receded.

CBOT is not the only outfit making this newfangled surgical equipment. In a *USA Today* story, five other companies were listed. The one most frequently mentioned in both the *USA Today* article and others is U.S. Surgical. In 1989 it had sales of over $342 million and net income of $30.6 million. On July 26 when Cabot hit 13¼, U.S. Surgical on the NYSE closed at 45½ with a price-to-earnings (P/E) ratio of 33. In contrast, on that same day, tiny Cabot (annual sales of $25 million) had a P/E of 70.

While the P/E for Standard & Poor's 500 Stock Index at that time was around 13 and the Dow Jones slightly less, the average P/E for this group of medical device companies was 37. Obviously, Cabot was out of line with the others in its industry. When it was down to 8⅞ it still had a P/E of 47.

Cabot's stock price wasn't helped when it came out with flat quarterly earnings, even though sales were up sharply.

President George G. Wood said that net income was penalized because marketing and sales activities were accelerated so that CBOT could capitalize on the new developments in the general surgery field.

That's a good management decision, for costs will be recouped further down the road. Unfortunately it didn't help the current stock price.

The selling by Cabot insiders is interesting.

Since we originally picked the stock in Jun '86, there have been only three times that insiders sold shares. President Wood, Chairman Harry Brener and Vice President Marvin Sharfstein sold comparatively small amounts at $2.44 in Jul '88. However, since the price began rising in May of this year, these three have sold twice.

In June and July these three officers collectively sold 615,000 shares. In July they received from $10 to $12 a share. We're sure that if they thought it was going much higher they would have waited until a later date. (Mr.

Wood and Mr. Brener still owned over one million shares each.)

A monthly advisory service that charges $129 a year recommended Cabot when it was $6.

It said that CBOT "is an aggressive buy up to $10 a share." This service also expected "earnings to be 48¢ to 52¢ a share with revenues doubling to $54 million."

Incidentally, we wonder why that $129-a-year investment newsletter didn't pick Cabot when it languished for years at under $3. At the $6 price it couldn't duplicate the 400% to 500% rise it experienced. . . . Oh well, it's fun to be catty once in awhile.

OUR SELECTION PROCESS

Fish gotta swim
Birds gotta fly
Nobody can tell you
What stocks you should buy

Even though we can't tell you what stocks to buy, maybe you would like to know the selection process used in picking our Company of the Month. . . . It's about time, you are probably saying.

In the three previous discussions in this series, we stressed the importance of diversification and selling. Not a word about selection.

Actually, we've hit you over the head ad nauseam about diversification. The lack of it is *Mistake No. 1* by minipricers.

However, some would quarrel with that and instead nominate "deciding exactly when to sell" as the *No. 1 Mistake*. It's certainly true that knowing when to sell can greatly improve the performance of your portfolio. Let us illustrate:

James Colby, Jr., of Peterborough, NH, got his son to buy Utah Medical when it was under $3. When it rose to $6, he wanted his offspring to sell half of his holdings. But, the son sold all at about $6. Utah Medical since then has been as high as 17¾. (As we hope you know by now, we say sell half of your holdings when they double in price and sell the other half when it backs down 25% from its most recent high.)

Picking a Winner

What we have been talking about is the mechanics of operating your portfolio. Now we'll get into selectivity. Many would contend we should have discussed that first. For some, just selecting a stock is all there is to equity investing.

We can't deny that choosing the right stock is vital. Obviously, if you pick only losers, you are not going to get anywhere. That would really sour you on the market.

So—how do we select stocks?

First of all, we do not like asset plays and concept stocks.

People will buy a company's shares even though it has not had a profit in five years. . . . Aha, they say, that's not important. Look at all of the assets (real estate, oil in the ground, patents, etc.)

There is a broker in San Diego who gives us a ring every three or four years with what he thinks is a bang-up asset play. One that we have to put in the newsletter pronto. None of his suggestions have worked out.

However, more investors are captivated by concept stocks than asset plays. Incidentally, for you little buckaroos who have just dived into the wonderful world of equity investing—a concept is an idea, a dream, a new theory. It has not yet been accepted by the marketplace. (These are sometimes called "story stocks.")

At one time, Xerox's plain-paper copier was just a concept. But when it was offered to the public—well, as Paul Harvey says, you know "the rest of the story." A very successful "c" stock.

Why Do So Many Concept Stocks Fail?

Most are not successful. It's not that the ideas are goofy. Failure usually comes by improperly introducing the service or product to the market. Or, the company runs out of capital. Or, there is a technical flaw in the concept.

Earlier in the life of *The Bowser Report* we presented some concept stocks. And, were we burned!

SCI-PRO, Inc. was one. In 1980 it designed a computerized system for restaurants. An electronic cash register that could do the payroll, keep track of inventory, track seasonal trends, etc. And, the system cost only $20,000.

A great concept. The same thing was implemented later by MICROS Systems and others. But, SCI-PRO was forced into a liquidating bankruptcy. Lack of capital and poor management did it in.

Hype, Hype, Hype

Concept stocks are sometimes heavily promoted. We certainly saw that with Twistee Treat—a kiosk in every shopping mall parking lot selling ice cream. The guy behind that was a promotional genius. But, alas! Twistee Treat is no longer with us.

One that made the rounds began in Nashville, TN. An old recording studio was acquired. It had some of Elvis Presley's first recordings, plus that of some other country music stars. . . . Action! Camera! Millions were about to be made. That was about a year ago.

The company is on the Vancouver Stock Exchange (a hotbed for concept stocks). It was supposed to be listed on Nasdaq. It still isn't. The firm makes a little money—but very little. It does have a promotion-minded president and a Houston stockbroker who is hyping the stock to high heaven. . . . The stocks we do recommend are risky enough without picking some based on hot air. However, in the overall scheme of things, it should be possible for a start-up company with a new theory to get equity capital. If one of these concept stocks really clicks, it can be a bonanza. However, for us, statistically they just do not work out.

How Do We Select Stocks?

At the beginning of each month we start with a stack of 20 to 25 folders. That stack comes from our research department, which monitors incoming information. Furthermore, we are aided by the screening for our sister publication, *Bowser's Directory of Small Stocks*.

During the month we live with those folders, each one containing information on one stock. Each is a potential Company of the Month. Daily the stock price is posted on all 20/25 stocks.

The companies in those folders usually have these features:

Profitable. Ideally we would like for them to have been in the black for the last five years. But, that is asking quite a bit for a company in our price category. If, in the last two or three years they have had a down year, we want a good explanation for it.

Capitalization. The smaller the number of shares outstanding, the better. After all—the price of a stock is the result of supply and demand. If there is a scramble to find shares to buy, that'll drive up the stock.

Future. What are the prospects? Is it in a growing field, or one that is stagnant? When you buy shares, you're betting on the firm's prospects for the next one, two or five years.

Market Makers. If it's on Nasdaq, we know from experience that the greater the number of brokers who are daily buying and selling shares for their clients, there is more likely to be a small spread between the bid and ask price.

Bowser Requirements. Each has to have our rating of 8 or better and be quoted daily in *The Wall Street Journal*. We aren't trying to sell *The Journal*. We just want one common place where a quote is available daily.

Speaking of the Bowser Ratings, they are not like the Value Line ones. We don't claim that the higher the number, the greater the chance for appreciation. However, since the ratings are based primarily on balance sheet items, a higher rating does indicate the corporation is stronger financially.

Market Chatter. We have a great respect for the market. What is it telling us about these stocks? Is the price of a particular stock going down or up? If down, there must be something negative that we don't know. If the price is ascending, investors think highly of the stock. As they say, "Don't fight the tape."

Finally, having done all of our homework. Having found a stock that fits our parameters precisely. That doesn't mean we automatically have a winner.

A month after we pick a company, management may make a lulu of a mistake in judgment. Or, external factors beyond the control of management spoil everything. That seems to happen frequently with the energy industry.

Nevertheless, if we can have as good a batting average in picking winners as Joe DiMaggio did in hitting baseballs, you, as well as ourselves—golly, if we just have a 300% average and that includes some big home runs, that'll make us happy.

WHAT SHOULD YOU DO IN A BEAR MARKET?

Specifically, what will happen to minipriced stocks in a bear market? They'll drop. Just like most of the other stocks. However, maybe not as much, because they don't have as far to slip. (In 1973-74, Coca-Cola was down 70%; McDonald's, 72%; Avon, 87%, and Walt Disney, 86%.)

The worst thing you can do is to panic. And, sell. . . . It'll be tempting. You'll hear a lot of gloomy talk and might think, the bear will reign supreme forever. . . . You'll be depressed, seeing your stocks plummet. We know. We went through the 1973-74 debacle.

Don't try to time it. That's a sucker's game. . . . One day it'll dawn on you that it is no fun looking at the stock tables. But, buckaroos, there is a light at the end of the tunnel. *Kiplinger's Personal Finance Magazine* notes that the 14 bear markets since 1926 did not last forever. The average was 16 months.

Just hold on. Don't sell just because the market is down. Then you'll be guaranteed to have a loss. After all, don't forget you are a long-term investor; and, willing to hold a stock many moons, if you think it still has potential. Remain fully invested.

No matter what five-year period you pick, mutual funds have always lagged the market. Funds are a good way to go, if you choose wisely. But individual stocks are by far the most proven road to riches.

—*Personal Finance*, 10/23/91

"The average mutual fund beat the S&P 500 only one year out of the last eight. This contradicts the argument that individual investors don't stand a chance against professionals," says Don Phillips, publisher of *Morningstar*, a publication that tracks mutual fund performance.

—The Wall Street Journal, 3/27/92

✦

EXPECTING TOO MUCH?

Men are different from women. (Have you noticed?) Elephants are different from mice. Minipriced stocks are different from blue chips.

Some, though, expect small stocks to perform the same as well-established, prosperous household names. Like Coca-Cola.

Sure, many, many decades ago Coca-Cola was a small company. But, only a few tiny outfits have grown to colossal proportions. Even in this capitalistic country.

Just go through stock market records of 40 years ago and you'll see many names of firms that have found their way to the small stock graveyard.

There are thousands of these little companies hidden in every nook and cranny of this nation. If they all became billion-dollar corporations, they'd be as omnipresent as 7-11s. Furthermore, they're risky. Many are poorly managed by highly-paid executives.

In our many years playing with these corporate babies, we have observed that only a handful have moved from under $3 a share to more than $25. Most are doing well if they get up to $6 or $7. And, even though there are hordes that never rise above $3 to $4, your chances of succeeding will increase if you do what we tell you to do.

With our personal portfolio, we have demonstrated the principles that you need to follow. . . . In this series we have been discussing them. . . . Now let's elaborate some more.

Expectations

We have been talking about having unrealistic hopes. Of expecting each of your minipriced purchases to be a home run. Actually, you can do very well with singles and doubles. Maybe, if you're fortunate, you'll get a three-bagger.

Cockeyed expectations take their most virulent form when someone buys 10,000 shares of one stock. And, that's all the money he or she has. . . . That is not investing. That's gambling. It's the I'm-going-to-make-a-killing syndrome.

If you look at the details of our portfolio—at all of the transactions—you'll see that our average gain was from $200 to $400. And, you'll note that the losses have been comparatively small. Too, in many instances, we've held the stocks for some time.

Reluctance to Sell

"The hardest thing for me to do is to learn to sell. I've had to do that since I started taking *The Bowser Report*." This is what one subscriber told us.

John Steele Gordon, in *American Heritage*, wrote: "Investors, like everyone else, are condemned to live their lives on the knife edge between the future that can never be foreseen and the past that can never be revisited."

And, it's the future that prevents many from selling a stock that has gone sour. They are convinced it will recover. They're really hoping for a turnaround, thus vindicating their decision to buy the stock in the first place.

Then there's the most frequently heard excuse: "It's down so much, I wouldn't get anything for it. Maybe I would not get enough to pay the commission."

Our reply: "Nonsense." In all our years, there have been only two or three, at the most, that dropped so much there was not enough for the brokerage fee by the time we recommended they be sold.

Most important is that you get rid of the dogs and move onto something with better prospects. But, we've known subscribers who refuse to sell. Consequently, they primarily own losers.

By refusing to sell when we suggested they do so, they've given up any money they would have received if they'd sold them. Besides, keeping these rotten equities in your basket poisons your entire approach to the market. You're constantly reminded of your failures.

We have already indicated how you should handle our stocks that have doubled and then some.

Right Price

Believe it or not, even in the narrow price range in which we work, there is a difference. The higher-priced stocks do better.

At the top of page 5 (Follow-Through) in the July 1991 *Bowser Report*, there were 28 stocks that had moved above $3. Of those 28, 25 were between $2 and $3 when we first recommended them. On the other hand, of the three that were under $2, they were between $1.50 and $2 when initially picked. None were under $1.

The moral is obvious. The higher-priced issues do better. So, you should keep that in mind when buying our stocks.

Unfortunately, some readers only buy the cheapest of the cheap, concentrating on those securities that are under $1. . . . And so, you might ask, why have them on the list?

We keep the really cheap ones on the list for two reasons: (1) Even though most have slipped from a higher price, they continue to be viable and there is no reason, based on fundamentals, to eliminate them. (2) Occasionally, some of these low-low-priced babies appreciate 100% or 200%.

Just keep in mind that statistically you'll do better with the stocks in the $2 to $3 range.

Following Our Advice

Frequently we'll ask a subscriber how many stocks he or she has. They'll recite a list that may include only two or three of our issues. Among the others they own, quite frequently, will be stocks we've never heard of.

For the Bowser Plan to be effective, you have to use our recommendations. That way you can keep tab on the latest developments in these companies and how we assess this information.

We aren't trying to dictate what stocks you should own. But, we do think it is only fair to yourself and to us, that you have a separate portfolio dedicated just to our equities. Otherwise, you won't get the benefit of the Bowser Plan.

Knowledge

You can make more money by owning stocks directly, rather than through mutual funds. Jordan Goodman, the *Money* magazine whiz, testified to that when we profiled him. But—and there always seems to be a "but"—you have to know what you're doing.

In any activity—be it your job, playing golf or tennis or chess—whatever you do, the more you know about the activity, the better. The same applies to buying and selling stocks outright.

This was succinctly enunciated by Philip John Neimark, editor of *Pro Trade* and the *Low-Priced Stock Edition*:

"Quite simply, if you are willing to devote the same time and energy to the stock market that you devote to your business or to the selection of a new car, if you are willing to learn a few rules and have the discipline to exercise them, and if you are willing to identify and follow professional advice, then you have a good chance to welcome yourself into the world's most exclusive club: the winners."

NO ONE IS ALWAYS RIGHT

(The following was excerpted from the July 8, 1991 issue of the *Dick Davis Digest*.)

A stock that is strongly recommended in confident, no-hedge language by an advisor with a good record and a national reputation that subsequently falls sharply in price can trigger deep feelings of resentment.

"He should have known! For this advice we have to pay money?!" But, this is nothing new.

It has always been thus—and always will be, as long as there are brave souls who attempt to make a living trying to predict the unpredictable.

What we must not lose sight of is that all of us are trying to be winners in a game where nobody has all the answers and where nobody is consistently right. The corollary of that truism is that everybody—repeat, everybody—will be wrong. And, if they play the game long enough, they will be wrong often.

In terms of advisors picking stocks—many of us have to lower expectations to the realities of the game we are playing.

If we know ahead of time it is going to be difficult to be a consistent winner, we should not be surprised or even angry when we actually experience those difficulties.

No one likes to lose money—but we sometimes think that if investors were better educated about what to expect in the "battle of investment survival," there would be less pain.

The slick, high-powered "hype" and exaggerated claims of some market letters and a minority of stock salesmen often cause the gullible public to enter the market arena with totally unrealistic expectations.

(*Dick Davis Digest*, PO Box 9547, Fort Lauderdale, FL 33310-9547, 305/771-7111, 24 times yearly, $165.00.)

From both the standpoint of the national interest and individual self interest, I think individual ownership of stock is the best buy year in and year out that you are going to find. Of course. the market will be up and down, but if an individual will take a longer-term view, I think individual ownership of stocks is as good as you'll get.

— James R. Jones

"THESE ARE NOT JUNK STOCKS"

Paul Kamke is a busy certified public accountant, with his own practice. But, he took the time to talk to us in December 1993.

Bowser: What has been the history of your stock market experience?

Kamke: I was interested in stocks when I was 12 years old. My uncle was a big fan of *Value Line.* I remember reading *Value Line* at his house when I was 12 years old. That was my first real exposure.

Do you remember the first stock you bought?

I can't remember the name, but do remember I lost all of my money in it.

All of your money?

All of my money. I think it was Aircraft International. It was something with aircraft in the name. It had something to do with the Vietnam War.

How much did you lose?

About $1,000.

That was a pretty rocky start.

From then on my father would periodically buy some stocks. Mostly those that paid dividends. I would be researching those stocks, even when I was in high school.

Did you ever take a course in stocks?

> In high school you had to be a senior to take a stock class. But, I managed to get in as a sophomore.

How did you do in that class?

> I had the highest grade in the class. I was just technically oriented towards that sort of thing. The same way with accounting.

When did you actually buy another stock?

> When I was 18, I bought a couple of small stocks.

How did they do?

> On one I made a profit. The other was a loser.

When did you get into the market in a bigger way?

> Max, my real introduction to the market, or, to put it more specifically, to small stocks, was when I found *The Bowser Report.* I remember my roommate and myself called you from college to ask about certain stocks. And, that's what really got me started.

Since you were a college student, money must have been a problem.

> I didn't have much, but when I did have some extra, I'd buy one of your stocks.

Remember any of them?

> School Pictures was one of them. I made 100% profit on it. That was in the early 1980s, before you had your Selling Plan.

Did you ever buy Telefonos de Mexico?

I know you're one of the first to ever recommend Telefonos. I've owned that one about five times.

Did you make a profit each time?

Every time.

Do you own it now?

Yes.

As an accountant, I guess you like to get the annual reports and quarterlies and check out the figures yourself.

Originally I did. But, after awhile, I said, "This is ridiculous." I automatically buy your recommendations now. You're going to do more research than I'm ever going to do.

We're sure you've had some losers.

There are only two of your stocks I have owned that have gone under. One you told us to sell, which was Chipwich. The other was a special situation stock you had years and years ago.

Paul, what's the biggest loser in your current portfolio?

Ajay Sports. It's down 77%.

Do you tell people about *The Bowser Report?*

Yes. I tell them about Transmedia Network. I'll tell them about Three-Five Systems. But, then, they'll ask, "How about the losers?" I say, "Of course, there are losers. But, I've never had one that was a total loss. They seem to think all low-priced stocks are worthless."

How do you feel about the losers?

A Three-Five Systems or a Transmedia can make up for a lot of losers.

How do you keep up with your portfolio?

I have it on a computer and post it every day or whenever I have the time.

Who is your broker?

Fidelity Discount.

How have you been doing with your Bowser stocks?

In 1990, I was up just over 5%. In 1991, over 130%. In 1992, 76%. This year, in the 60% range. I've done tremendously well.

Do you follow our Selling Plan?

When they drop 25% from their most recent high, I sell. For example, Spectran and Transmedia aren't in the portfolio anymore, because they dropped 25% from their high.

How much of your own money is invested in Bowser stocks?

Around $12,000.

How much have you made on that $12,000?

Over $60,000.

As an accountant, you deal with your clients on a fiduciary basis. How do you reconcile dealing with minipriced stocks that many consider speculative?

The way I do it, I say, "I've been subscribing since the early 1980s. I've followed this whole thing. Send away for it. It's only $48. It's not going to break your bank. Look at the Company of the Month selection. I can attest to you that he's telling the truth. You can look at a mutual fund's past performance, but you can't tell what will happen with it in the future. The same with these stocks."

How would you characterize our stocks?

These are not junk stocks. These are not stocks on the Vancouver Stock Exchange. These are legitimate companies. You've had some big names. I remember that at one time you had Pier 1 Imports.

How much of one's investment funds should go into minipriced stocks?

I don't think they should be 100% of someone's retirement plan. They could be a good portion. I have them geared up to be 30% of my pension plan.

Now are you buying each Company of the Month?

Regardless. Automatically. But, that's only in the last year. Previously, I did not have enough money. From 1990 until a year ago, I'd buy about 8 of the 12 yearly Companies of the Month.

What do you think of our Game Plan?

I think it's very intelligent. I remember years ago listening to a chap on the radio who advocated selling after they'd dropped 10% from their most recent high. But, he was dealing in higher-priced stocks. You are saying 25% after a stock doubles. So, you aren't then dealing with a $2 stock. It's usually $5 or $6 at that point.

Suppose you buy a stock at $3. It goes to $6. You sell half. It gets up to $10, then drops back to $7.50. You sell the last of your shares. A year later, that stock is $25. . . . What do you do? Cry? Kick your dog, or what?

You can't cry over investments that might have been. I wanted to sell IBM when it was 110 last year and we were building our house. I can't cry now that it is $55. You've got to go onto the next investment. There's always another stock that's going to go up. You could've hit lotto if you'd changed one number.

What would you do if we had a really bad bear market? I don't mean one like 1929, but one like 1973-74, that lasted two years.

Which I haven't lived through. I read that most of today's money managers haven't lived through a real bear market. . . . You know what I would do? I would not stop investing in stocks. Because, in a bear market, there are always companies that perform well. In the 1980s, when small stocks were being clobbered, you always had winners.

In social gatherings, what reaction do you get from your friends when you tell them you're buying stocks $3 a share or less?

They think I'm crazy.

They do?

> I can't tell you the number of people to whom I've mentioned *The Bowser Report*. But, I only know of one who actually subscribed.

What's their big objection?

> They think these stocks are too risky. For me, I look at the records of the average mutual fund managers; and, my record is better than theirs. But, I'm getting more acceptance now that I can point out Transmedia. A lot of people have heard of Transmedia. With their stock split, my cost price for Transmedia was 1⅛. Oddly enough, many think you aren't any good, because the price of your newsletter is so low.

What do you look for in a stock? You probably like some of our picks better than others.

> I like technological issues. I think that anything with technology has a chance to be tremendous if it comes through.

How about some that you were a little queasy about?

> Ajay Sports I didn't really like. But, I am a golfer, so I said, "What the heck?" Besides, I had seen some of their products.

In an annual report, what do you look for?

> I don't like debt. I've never liked debt. A small number of shares outstanding is also very important to me. Another thing is, "How are they controlling general administrative expenses?" A company can't,

for example, control cost of goods. That's the result of supply and demand. But, they can control administrative expenses. If they keep going up as a percentage of sales, that really bothers me.

Do you have a great deal of patience? Are you willing to sit with a stock three or four years?

Definitely.

Do you believe in market timing?

It almost never works.

How much time do you devote each week to your stock investments?

I check on them every day. Including reading financial publications, about six to seven hours a week.

THE PAUL KAMKE FILE

Business: Paul B. Kamke, CPA, 2 Crossfield Avenue, Suite 210, West Nyack, NY 10994, 914/358-4677.

Born: 1959, Mount Vernon, New York.

Education: Graduated in 1981 from the University of Virginia, receiving a degree in commerce, with a concentration on accounting.

Career: Peat Marwick Mitchell (now (KPMG), then to Citicorp, where he learned about computers. Became self-employed four years after college. Has frequently spoken on the radio and at seminars. Had his own newsletter, *Paul Kamke's Investment & Tax Alert.*

Personal: Married Gail Foster in Sep'90. Two children.

Hobbies: Golf, plays in many amateur and local professional events.

WHY DOES MERRILL LYNCH
HATE $2 STOCKS?

The giants of this business don't like small companies—that is, if their stock happens to be $3 or less. We're talking about the big wire houses, such as Merrill Lynch, Dean Witter, Bear Stearns, etc. Plus some large regional firms.

Why do these brokerage Goliaths have such a bias against minipriced issues? After all, it's generally recognized that these tiny companies are the biggest creators of jobs in the country. But, this segment of Wall Street has no interest in nurturing them. For that, these companies have to rely on smaller brokerages and investment bankers.

Walk into one of these big brokerages to buy a $2 stock and you'll get the idiot treatment. Here are some of the excuses they'll give for not buying the little stocks. And, the real reason they don't want to buy them.

Factor No. 1

Risk. "Speculative" is the first word that comes from the broker's lips. Ignored is the fact that all stocks are speculative to a certain degree. And, these are the same people who will sell you options, futures, CMOs (collateralized mortgage obligations), etc. These are the same people who have sold worthless real estate partnerships. These are the same people who sold speculative derivatives to unsophisticated public treasurers across the country.

Factor No. 2

"If we recommended a $2 stock, we'd drive up the price beyond reason." . . .That's what they said about Three-Five Systems when it was below $3. But, when it was $35 a share, every big brokerage was recommending it. When we picked TFS in May '91, it had around 3.5 million shares. Now, after a 2-for-1 split, it has less than 8 million—still a comparatively small number. If the big brokerage recommendations would run up the stock at $2, why didn't they run it up from $35 to $100?

Factor No. 3

Those who don't like low-priced stocks will frequently say, *"They are at that price for a reason."* That's supposed to be the knock-out argument. . . . Of course, there's a reason every stock is at a given price. The trick is to find out why the stock is $2. And then try to determine if there are indications it will perform better in the future.

Factor No. 4

"We might be sued if we recommend a speculative $2 stock." We have faithfully read the financial press for years and we don't recall a brokerage being taken to court because a $2 stock went to $1 or even to zero. . . . While the general public may not understand derivatives

and CMOs and all aspects of options—they do know they are taking a chance with a $2 stock.

Factor No. 5

You've heard the expression "politically correct." *The flip side is "economically correct."* With some, there is almost a cultural bias against low-priced equities. In this country, high-priced stocks have long been favored. In contrast, in most foreign countries, investors prefer low-priced issues.

Factor No. 6

All penny stocks are scams. It's true that small unethical brokers sell worthless penny stocks. But, the SEC, the National Association of Securities Dealers and state regulators have taken measures to greatly clean up this mess. But, to use a broad brush and paint all low-priced stocks as scams is just as unreasonable as calling all brokers crooks. But, we're sure that when Three-Five Systems was $2.50 a share, there were brokers at the big houses calling it "junk."

Factor No. 7

There's no information on these little companies. . . . The big brokers may not have the information in their offices, but these firms would be glad to supply it. . . . These brokers don't have the necessary annual and quarterly reports, etc., simply because they or their research departments have no interest in collecting this material.

Factor No. 8

"*I would like to sell you that $2 stock, but my firm won't let me. I'll see if my branch manager will OK your purchasing this highly speculative and dangerous stock.*" Many firms don't want anyone to think they even have the slightest association with inexpensive issues. We were going to interview an outstanding broker at A. G. Edwards & Sons, but the firm would not let him participate in the interview. Why? Because it would appear in a newsletter featuring "cheap stocks."

Factor No. 9

"*Our research department doesn't follow those cheap stocks.*" Marvin Roffman, the Janney Montgomery Scott casino analyst, who was booted from his job for saying bad things about Trump's Atlantic City gambling empire, wrote a book, *Take Charge of Your Financial Future* (Birch Lane Press, New York). In it, Mr. Roffman says that at the big firms, analysts are paid to bring in institutional customers with big bucks. They'd have difficulty finding "big bucks" in the stocks of little companies.

Factor No. 10

In Factor No. 9, we're beginning to touch on the real reason big brokerages don't want to deal in minipriced stocks. With a big overhead, their costs are so high they don't make money on a transaction of 200 shares of a $2 stock. And, to discourage this, they make sure the broker doesn't profit from one of these deals. Nor would they look upon such sales as "loss leaders." They aren't interested in working with a customer with the hope that in the future his business will be profitable. . . . *This, then, is the real reason they dislike little stocks. All of their other excuses are just bull manure.*

LET'S TALK
PORTFOLIO MANAGEMENT

We hear from our subscribers. Frequently. By mail. By fax. By phone.

Questions. Questions. And, some call to compliment. . . . Sometimes they call to complain. Because they're losing. Losing is no fun.

When we do have an opportunity to examine in detail a few of those losing situations, we usually find poor portfolio management.

In building your portfolio, the first factor to consider is QUANTITY. After you have picked a stock. . . . How many are you going to buy? . . . This is where greed sometimes comes in. "The more I buy, the more I'll make."

Initially, you should take a small position in one of our stocks. They do bounce around. Maybe they spike up for a transitory reason. Another newsletter or a brokerage firm recommends one of them. That is an artificial stimulus.

After awhile they will settle back. You don't want to buy when they have spiked up. Improving performance is the only engine that drives up a stock price and keeps it up.

Datawatch was a Company of the Month. At the time we wrote it up, the price was 2¹¹⁄₁₆. However, while the newsletter was at the printer and in the mail, the price jumped to 3⅜. On Monday and Tuesday, after publication, it could have been bought for 3⅜.

In our recorded message, on the weekend following publication, we suggested you take a small position, even though DWCH was over 3. Based on previous experience, we know a stock like this can fall back. However, as we write this, Datawatch did fall to under $3.

Some might say, "I was going to buy 1,000 shares, but I only bought 200 because of what you said on the recording. You've caused me to 'lose' money because now it's 3⅞."

This is a line of reasoning that baffles us. In the situation we just outlined, some might think they "lost" money, but it's our experience you can't buy anything with that kind of currency. . . . On the other hand, if DWCH was now 2½, we hope they would credit us with "saving" them money.

In Feb '94, we published, in our Subscriber's Forum, a Texan's portfolio. He had purchased 27 Bowser stocks for $34,905.23. . . . From time to time we've been checking on the portfolio's progress. But, it's a discouraging experience.

To begin with, he made most of the purchases on the Monday following our publication. Consequently, much of the time he was paying the maximum price. Secondly, he bought 600 to 1,000 shares of each issue. He didn't reserve any of his funds for possibly averaging down.

WE THINK IT IS OK TO AVERAGE DOWN IF THE FUNDAMENTALS REMAIN THE SAME.

We don't suggest averaging *up* with minipriced stocks. When they do well, most of them only climb to $6, $8 or $10. Consequently, you'd be investing and getting little gain.

We do, though, have some that turn into super stocks. But, when they are just $3, you're a better person than we if you can select those that will top out over $15. . . . In Dec '94, when you could have bought Semtech for $2.50, we had no idea that in May '95 it would get up to $60.

The second factor to consider in portfolio management is TIME. It can be your friend. Or, your enemy.

We hear frequently that common stocks are one of the best investments—if not the very best—you can make. Long term. Short term they can be disastrous; Las Vegas could be a better bet.

Why? You can blame the liquidity of stocks. You can buy one and sell it minutes later. Try that with real estate. This very liquidity encourages some investors to have a short-term view.

In fact, no other investment form has the liquidity of stocks. Because of this, many equity investors have unrealistic expectations. They want sensational results quickly.

If a stock doesn't double in a year or two, they are ready to throw in the towel. They ignore the fact that it takes time for a company to develop.

And, back to the Texan with the $34,000 Bowser portfolio. In Oct '93, in a letter to us, he wrote that Scanforms, Inc. (Nasdaq:SCFM) was his pick to double in 12 months. It was then 2⅝. That's the highest it reached in 1994.

We aren't saying that Scanforms was a poor selection. Maybe it will eventually work out. Our point is that his statement it would "double in 12 months," indicates he thinks short term.

In portfolio management, the third factor we are considering is DISCIPLINE. In our case, it means following the Bowser Game Plan, which every subscriber should know by heart.

The chief advantage of having the discipline to follow a game plan is that it removes emotions from your decision making. Especially in the critical area of selling. Which, in many cases, determines the success or failure of a portfolio.

A stock doubles, you sell half of your holdings. It crawls up to 10, but slips back to 7½, a 25% decline from its high. Then, that old emotion, Mr. Greed, whispers that the stock will get back to 10. But, you sell at 7½. Later it collapses to less than 3.

That's almost exactly what happened to Cascade International, the fraud-ridden clothing retailer. It doubled and shot up to over 11 and then began to decline. . . . Just recently, a subscriber called and, among other things, mentioned he'd made money on Cascade because he followed our game plan.

The Texan we've been talking about . . . he had 600 shares of Semtech. . . . With that one stock his gain could have been great enough to cover most of the losers. But, he didn't follow our selling plan. He sold all 600 at one time and very early. He missed most of Semtech's big advance. . . . QUANTITY, TIME, DISCIPLINE. Three words that can lead to successful minipriced stock investing.

HAVE A WINNING MIND-SET

The following was written by ROD FADEM, a senior vice president with Oppenheimer & Co. in St. Louis. It appeared in the July 18, 1994 Barron's.

In Mar '87, two of my clients each bought 1,000 shares of Scitex, an Israeli company, at 7¾. Ultimately, one lost over $5,000 and the other made $500,000. How can this be?

The answer is simple and holds lessons for other investors. One of the clients had a winner's mentality; the other, regrettably, a loser's.

In Oct '87, the Crash hit and Scitex was battered down to $2. Client A, appalled by the headlines and emotionally spent, ordered me to "get rid of the dog."

He never asked if something had changed with the company or if a buying opportunity had been created by the overall market decline. When the stock rallied to $6, I called him back, suggesting he consider repurchasing because it was too low in relation to its fundamentals.

"How can I buy it at $6 when I sold it at $2?" he replied.

His hangup about the price wouldn't allow him to assess the situation calmly and buy back Scitex, so he missed out on a lucrative opportunity.

Client B, on the other hand, asked if the company's fundamentals had suddenly deteriorated. I answered no, that while Scitex was losing money, this was certainly nothing new and that its prospects still appeared good. The company's products were highly regarded and there was hope for a turn around.

After examining the latest quarterly and annual reports, he bought another 1,000 shares at 2½. He subsequently bought more whenever the stock made a new high.

He held through the crises of the 1991 Gulf War and a myriad of bearish rumors. By Nov '92, Scitex had hit 39. Client B sold. He had made $500,000.

What made A a loser and B a winner? Different mind-sets.

A PROFILE IN PATIENCE
STEVE SICKELS

We interviewed Lt..Col.(Ret) Sickels at his home in the Boston area on Nov. 18, 1995.

Bowser: How did you find out about *The Bowser Report?*

> *Sickels:* I was interested in the stock market. Had read a few books on it and didn't know where to go to get further information. But, in 1980, I did go to a Merrill Lynch broker and this guy said I ought to look at this service that gives you all of these sample newsletters.

Select Information Exchange?

> That's the one. SIE.

What else did the Merrill Lynch broker tell you?

> He said, "By the way, I know you're interested in small stocks—I can't do any here at Merrill Lynch—but you can make money in them. You should ask for *The Bowser Report* through SIE." So, I did that. And, after I got the sample copy, I subscribed.

How did you become interested in the stock market in the first place?

> I saw it as an opportunity to make money by being willing to take a risk.

If you wanted to take risk, why not Las Vegas?

> My studies helped lead me to stocks. You see, I was getting a master's degree in research and development management at the time.

You were in the U.S. Air Force then?

> Yes. I was a captain. And, in the process of working on that degree, I had to study finance and accounting. I learned how to read a balance sheet.

But, you didn't have a lot money, did you?

> No. That is one reason *The Bowser Report* is so great. It doesn't cost much to buy shares. And, you can diversify.

When you started, you didn't buy 12 different Bowser stocks in one day—did you?

> No. Let me add that since 1980 I've worked with three or four brokers and consistently lost on their advice. Yet, with *The Bowser Report*, although the 1980s were lean years, the 1990s have been the best and 1995 was phenomenal.

So, how do you feel overall about your experience with minipriced stocks?

> If someone could have told me in the 1980s what was going to happen, I would have put more money into Bowser stocks.

Initially, then, you just bought one or two. Later, you bought more when you could afford to. Right?

Yes.

That's a great way to get started, particularly for a young person. However, what frequently happens is that the first one or two stocks don't do well and he or she becomes discouraged and proclaims to the world, "You can't make money buying stocks."

My first two stocks were not huge successes.

Why did you continue?

Part of the reason I hung on was because I enjoyed the newsletter. I also realized I was a lousy stock picker and that I needed help.

How have you done in the market, overall, with Bowser stocks?

In the 1980s, I just broke even. In the 1990s, I have probably gone up 400%.

That is just with Bowser stocks?

Yes. As I previously told you, in the last 15 years I've used three or four brokers. But, if I had shorted the stocks they recommended, I would have been even richer.

Do you feel comfortable having most of your liquid assets in Bowser stocks?

Absolutely.

Now that you're entering a retirement period, will your investment activities change?

Not at all.

Computers have been an important part of your life, both in the Air Force and as a hobby. Have they helped you in your investment activities?

Absolutely.

How?

In two aspects. One, through using *The Bowser Directory* disk and with some dBase program commands, I can sift through *The Directory* and pick out those stocks with a low number of shares and with increasing earnings.

What is the other aspect?

CompuServe, for example, not only gives you quotes, but also news of the 700 to 800 companies in *The Directory*. Things such as earnings, insider selling, new product announcements, etc.

Have you bought some stocks from *The Directory*?

Yes. And, incidentally, I have bought about a half dozen that you later picked as Companies of the Month.

Any other comments on *The Directory*?

I'm impressed with the effort you make to maintain it. You are taking out those issues that have been delisted. And, you are always adding new ones. That is always fuel for more news and research. So, it is a living document. It's not static. I look forward each month to seeing what the new stocks are and their Bowser ratings.

What is the worst investment mistake you've made?

Security Environmental, without a doubt. I had about 2,000 shares. That is a company I bought on news before you recommended it.

What's the best investment decision you've made?

Three-Five Systems. I bought 500 between 2 and 3 and 1,000 for less than 2.

What is the advice you would give someone who is just starting with Bowser stocks?

I would say looking at the stocks too closely in relatlonship to their price is not good.

What do you mean?

There have been stocks that I watched for two or three years and then they doubled—this was before your selling plan. So, I said to myself, "I'm tired of watching this stock," and I sold after they doubled.

How about an example?

MICROS Systems. This is a company that you first selected in 1981. I sold immediately after it doubled. [MICROS Systems is now a $45 stock.]

Anything else?

As you suggest, diversification is important.

How many Bowser stocks do you have?

More than 50.

Anything else you'd recommend to the beginner?

Be patient. For example, I've had Mining Services Int'l ever since you recommended it in 1990. It has only gone up a point a year, on average. But, it's a successful long-term holding. . . . Too, investing should be fun. It certainly has been for me.

Steve, how about selling?

I've done a terrible job of selling.

Do you follow our selling plan?

Max, I try to at times. But, I guess that I think the 25 drop is too small. If it's a good company, they'll eventually keep going up. But, as I look at Three-Five Systems and some others, I see that my logic is wrong.

Didn't you own Halsey Drug? That's one where our selling plan would have salvaged you.

That got up as high as 11. Now, most of the time, it's below 3. Your selling plan would have worked on that one. . . . It's all a matter of discipline. Sometimes I don't have the discipline.

What do you think of the Bowser Game Plan?

I think that overall the idea of buying and holding and diversification is good. I think that the Game Plan is based on your experience over a long term. I think that's real wisdom. I can remember in the 1980s and other times, if a stock doubled—that was magnificent. Now, it seems like they quadruple or even more. This market is the exception. The way the market is going now, I've never seen anything like it—for minipriced stocks.

What's your criteria for buying?

I like to see the earnings turning around and usually—even if the company is losing money—that their losses are getting smaller. Again, I'm willing to take more risk than you do. I know that you always want the company to be profitable.

How much time do you spend each day on stocks?

Twenty to thirty minutes.

How many shares do you buy at a time?

I like to buy 1,000 to 1,500.

Why?

When I first started, I only bought a couple hundred shares. Now I can afford to buy more.

What is the best part of *The Bowser Report?*

You and Cindy and the unsung heroes on your staff.

THE STEVE SICKELS FILE

Born: Los Angeles in 1949.

Education: UCLA, majored in physical sciences and math. Has two masters' degrees.

Career: Joined the U.S. Air Force after getting a degree at UCLA. Graduated from Officer Training School in 1972. Pilot training at Webb AFB in Big Springs, Texas. Had survival training at three different bases. Flew C-130s. Arrived in the Philippines in April '74. Participated in the Saigon, Vietnam evacuation. Flew for 10 years. Balance of career was devoted to program management. Worked on development of the B-1 and B-2 bombers and new systems for AWAC planes. Retired in 1995 with 23 years service and rank of lieutenant colonel.

Retirement Plans: Feels that God has watched over him. So, in his next career, he wants to serve God and humanity. He is now enrolled in a seminary. Expects to graduate in a couple of years. Plans to go into full-time ministry. Feels that because he has retirement pay, what he does from now on won't have to have a lot of money involved in it.

Personal: Married in 1976 in Taipei, Taiwan to Aileene Yee. Have two daughters. One is a freshman at Smith College and the other is a high school junior.

Hobbies: Computers, reading and walking.

BIG BROKERAGES WAR AGAINST SMALL COMPANIES

Small companies create jobs. Lots of jobs. . . . If we depended on big corporations, the unemployment rate would now be sky high.

It is estimated that two thirds of all new employment opportunities are created by small businesses. But, the nation's full-service brokerages do not want anything to do with small companies—if their stock's selling for less than $5 a share.

Ride into an office of one of these brokerage goliaths on a mule and wave a banner with the inscription, "I love $2 stocks." . . . They'd think you were eccentric. . . . Not because of the mule, but because you like $2 stocks.

We recently got an insight into this phobia about small stocks. In the Jan. 31 *Wall Street Journal* appeared a story about Reuben G. Taub, 38, a top Paine-Webber broker, who generated $2.6 million in commissions in 1995. He was a member of the firm's exclusive Chairman's Club.

Nevertheless, Mr. Taub was fired by Paine-Webber. . . . Why? Because, according to *The Journal,* "he allegedly violated trading restrictions in a small company stock for his wife's account." . . . Now, that is an example of blatant spousal abuse. . . . Would you want to live next door to a guy who put too many small-company stocks in his wife's account? Of course not.

And, it's interesting that according to *The Journal,* "Mr. Taub doesn't seem to have had past problems. A review of his disciplinary history turns up a relatively clean record." However, he was suspended for two business days for allegedly exceeding trading limits in an unidentified small-company stock—but, he was exonerated.

The guy, obviously, likes small stocks.

Nevertheless, we were surprised that Bear Stearns almost immediately hired Mr. Taub, even though this is another firm that is not a booster for minipriced stocks.

Why are these firms so touchy, touchy about small stocks?

To begin with, they'll tell you they do recommend small stocks—if they are priced $5 or better. (If a stock is $4.87, it's one of those dreaded "penny stocks." But, if the next day, it's $5, it's a marvelous little stock.)

On page 117 we discuss this subject—"Why does Merrill Lynch hate $2 stocks?" Then we listed several of the excuses given as to why they are scared of minipriced issues. . . . There are two prime ones.

In this litigious society, they're afraid someone will buy the stock of one of these tiny companies, which will shortly thereafter go into bankruptcy. The brokerage firm will be sued, with the lawyers contending that

Merrill Lynch or whoever should have known that the company was about to collapse.

Every day, hundreds of smaller brokerages sell many thousands of minipriced shares. We read the financial press religiously and extensively. We've never read of a securities firm being sued by an irate holder of small stocks.

Of course, these big firms are targeted by attorneys for selling risky partnerships, options, futures and derivatives. But, not over these tiny stocks. . . . This is just a smoke screen.

Another favorite excuse goes something like this: We are so big and have so many brokers that if we recommend one of these little companies, the stock price will skyrocket.

We wouldn't expect their head of research to get on the squawk box and tell all of their thousands of registered representatives to concentrate on selling Pro-Dex, Inc. Rather, we envision the research department isolating 30 or 40 minipriced issues with good fundamentals. If we can do it, they certainly could.

Consequently, when a hombre walks in and wants to buy a $2 stock, instead of giving him—or her—the idiot treatment, the broker would pull out his sheet with the 30 or 40 issues and pick a low-priced dandy.

But, getting back to this business of their recommending a stock and the price skyrockets. *Smart Money* did something akin to that. They highlighted seven stocks under $2. After the publication was distributed to its many hundreds of thousands of readers, the stocks did get a bounce. But, nothing dramatic. (See the box on page 142.)

There is only one reason why these huge security firms avoid low-priced equities. They make little money on them. If a fellow buys 200 shares of a $2 stock, that's only $400.

They want you to waltz into their offices with $200,000. $500,000 would be better. And, if you had $1,000,000, they'd give you a free cup of coffee.... Asset collection is the big thing. And, you can't accumulate many assets with $400 orders.

But, frankly, we don't know why we get so frothy at the mouth about this subject. These big wire houses are doing OK financially. And, right now they don't need the microcap business.... Too, this being a free country, they can sell whatever they want to.

What we object to is their demonizing these little companies. Their very existence is an essential part of our entrepreneurship system. And, in turn, we resent their trashing the readers of *The Bowser Report* because they have the fortitude and the risk tolerance for these little babies.

SMART MONEY BRAVELY SHOWS THAT $2 STOCKS CAN BE PROFITABLE

Major financial publications normally don't have a good word for minipriced stocks. They buy the orthodox thinking: a $2 stock is cheap for a reason. If it was any good, it would be $20 a share.

In June '94, *Smart Money* defied the experts. In a feature article, the magazine selected seven stocks, each of which was under $2, that they believed would appreciate nicely.

The magazine did bow to orthodoxy by saying that minipriced stocks are in "a netherworld inhabited by companies too small, too shaky and often too troubled to have much of a following among institutions or Wall Street analysts."

However, John H. Taylor, in his fair-minded article, did note: "Over the years, so-called microcaps—obscure stocks with market capitalizations of less than $20 million—have produced some of Wall Street's most eye-popping returns."

Mr. Taylor then proceeded to prove it is possible to identify worthwhile companies in this low priced category. . . . He called on Wilshire Associates, a California consulting firm, to sort through a universe of $2-and-under microcaps according to price-to-book ratio, five-year earnings growth and five-year return of equity. . . . Thus, they were able to identify 53 companies that appeared to have favorable possibilities.

Author Taylor culled those 53 down to seven. He said that most of the companies selected shared similar traits: a clear focus, solid balance sheet, have growth potential, and experienced management that owns a hefty chunk of the firm's stock.

In the table on the next page, we show those seven companies, their price in June '94 and in Feb '96.

Their performance, needless to say, was outstanding. Note the average gain of 194%. . . . In 1995, the average gain of the stocks, recommended by the big brokerages mentioned above, was only 35%, as noted in th 2/8/96 *Wall Street Journal.*

Instead of bad mouthing low-priced equities, Wall Street should have some of their 2,600 high-priced analysts pick a flock of good $2 stocks. But, that won't happen. Not enough profit for the big brokerages in these little buggers.

SMART MONEY'S SEVEN MICROCAP STOCKS

	JUN '94	2/26/96	INCREASE
LUXTEC CORP (AMEX:LXU)	$1.75	$4.00	129%
WESTERBEKE CORP (NASDAQ:WTBK)	1.50	3.00	100%
CARTENDERS HEALTH CORP (NASDAQ:CTND)	1.94	7.25	273%
RAWSON-KOENIG INC (NASDAQ:RAKO)	1.25	1.53	22%
COMTREX SYSTEMS CORP (NASDAQ:COMX)	.75	.38	-49%
XETA CORP (NASDAQ:XETA)	1.31	9.50	625%
ALPNET INC (NASDAQ:AILP)	.40	1.44	260%
		AVERAGE GAIN	1360%
			194%X

In Jun '94, all of the above were in *Bowser's Directory of Small Stocks*

NAVIGATING THROUGH
THE PENNY STOCK WATERS

We hear a lot of bad things about penny stocks. . . . Frequently they are pictured as being worthless companies that are heavily manipulated by unethical brokers. . . . In other words, if you have a deep desire to lose money, buy penny stocks. They are as risky as the devil.

Penny stocks? What's our definition? . . . Anything under a dollar. If you ask what is the price of a stock and you are told it's 25¢ a share. Or 50¢. Or 99¢. It's a penny stock. . . . That to us, is the correct definition.

But, many people in the investment world consider anything under $5 a share to be in the penny stock category. . . . Euphemistically, we like to call them "small stocks." Doesn't have the pejorative sound of "penny stocks."

And, now that we are talking small stocks—there is another way to identify them. That's by their capitalization, which is derived by multiplying the number of shares outstanding by the price per share. Thus, if a company has 5,000,000 shares and its stock is selling for $5, you have an outfit with a capitalization of $25,000,000.

Those who are prejudiced against these stocks apparently operate on the theory that all small companies are basically worthless and consequently have little in the way of a profitable future. . . . This is a thesis that that can be easily refuted.

At this point, let's bring in Dan Lufkin, one of the founders of the New York brokerage firm of Donaldson, Lufkin & Jenrette, Inc. . . . The year was 1959. . . . Dan was only 24. . . . He and his two partners only had $60,000 between them as capital for this new firm. Not a princely sum. Even in 1959.

We heard Dan tell his story to a spellbound audience at a New York City conference early in 1996. (The original partners are not active in the firm today. Dan is now a venture capitalist. William Donaldson was chairman of the New York Stock Exchange. Richard Jenrette earlier in 1996 retired as CEO of the Equitable Companies.)

In 1959, Donaldson, Lufkin & Jenrette decided to concentrate on small stocks. . . . At the same time, young Lufkin wrote a pamphlet called "Common Stock and Common Sense." And, in it, he argued that to get an uncommon relatively high return you should discover the institutional blue chips of tomorrow. "That meant looking where most investors are not looking—the OTC (Nasdaq Stock Market) and regional favorites."

Nevertheless, experts were warning him to stay away from those small stocks. They argued that they carried much greater investment risk and their float (number of shares available for daily trading) is limited, so less institutional ownership is feasible.

They also said that limited demand means less liquidity if you want to sell and less existing research—so you will know less.

Mr. Lufkin concedes that these criticisms by experts were correct to some extent. "As with most tenets in the investment field, it's not black or white," he noted. "The experts overlooked what can happen if you pick a quality small company or a loser that has been turned around. Your investment could explode as the income soars."

The latter reasoning is why Donaldson, Lufkin & Jenrette initially focused on smaller companies in the $5 million to $50 million sales range. Many had wonderful managements and great track records.

In short, we have so far noted the risks involved with small stocks and also the rewards. . . . The question then is, "When you're fishing in this ocean, how do you avoid the sharks and land the tunas?"

First of all, we have to get a handle on this risk thing. We certainly don't want to lose our money. Our goal is to make money. . . . Peter L. Bernstein has come to our rescue. He's written an excellent book—*AGAINST THE GODS, The Remarkable Story of Risk*. Therein he portrays the role that risk plays in the life of man, going back to 16th century Italy. And, through the years there were many theories on controlling risk. They paved the way for the development of modern portfolio theory, *which says that diversification reduces risk*. Harry

Markowitz put forth the theory at the age of 25 in a 1952 paper in the *Journal of Finance*.

This, then, brings us to our game plan—the blueprint for successfully investing in small stocks (i.e., penny stocks). . . . Our game plan has two essential elements.

The first element is the matter of diversification as a means of controlling our risk. We say that you should have 12 to 18 different stocks scattered through various industries.

Thus, since we specialize in stocks selling for $3 a share or less, you can buy 12 issues at an average price of $2 each for a total of only $4,800, ignoring commissions. At an average price of $3, the tab would only come to $7,200. . . . These are not huge sums in the world of investing.

The second element of our game plan involves selling—the most important function in the stock market investment cycle. As the old adage goes, you don't make or lose money until you sell.

We suggest you buy at least 200 shares (more if you can afford it) of each stock. Then, when the stock price doubles from what you paid for it, sell 100 shares or half of your holdings. That way you will have liquidated your costs. From then on, you're operating on other people's capital.

If the stock continues to climb, sell when it drops back 25% from its most recent high. For example, you bought 200 shares at $3. The stock doubled to $6. You sold 100 shares. It moves up and down for several weeks—or months. But, it hits $10 and then backs down to $7.50. That's a 25% retreat from its high. You sell. Your profit was $750. Plus you got back your original investment of $600. As a result, you have $1,350 that you can invest in what we call "minipriced stocks." In other words, you have harnessed the power of compounding. . . . We all know what good things that can lead to.

Obviously, not all of these babies are going to grow up and be big successes. Some flounder. And when they do, its important that you sell. You don't want dead wood in your portfolio. . . . In our newsletter, *The Bowser Report*, when we have one whose performance is subpar, we specifically tell our readers to sell. In 1996, we recommended the sale of three stocks.

How has this worked out? Has the game plan been executed with success? . . . We could give various examples. . . . There are a lot of them. . . . People who have successfully used the game plan.

First, let's tell you about Chuck Bostrom, who was the superintendent of schools in the little town of West Yellowstone, Montana, on the edge of the beautiful and famous Yellowstone National Park. . . . About four years ago, Chuck sold a house in another town for a profit of around $5,000. He took that money and began investing in Bowser minipriced stocks.

At every step of the way he followed the game plan. Today that $5,000 is worth $18,000. . . . He has not had to add to the kitty. His portfolio is self financing, in that he plows his profits back into the portfolio.

Let's go across the country to West Nyack, New York, where Paul Kamke, an accountant, has his office. . . . He has been interested in minipriced stocks ever since he was a student at the University of Virginia. But, in recent years, he has done very well in his practice. Enough so that he put $12,000 into stocks recommended in our newsletter. . . . The last time we talked with Paul, his portfolio was worth over $60,000. . . . He is a real promoter of the game plan (See page 108).

Finally, a word about commissions. . . . Some will say that you can't make money with penny stocks because the brokerage commissions will eat you up. . . . That might have had some validity when everything went through full-service brokers. Today, though, discount brokers, particularly the deep discount variety, have driven down brokerage fees to the point that they are a minor consideration. Even a full-service broker will give you a break if you buy in big enough quantities.

GREED:
THE EIGHTH DEADLY SIN

Man is a bundle of emotions. They make us function as human beings. Of the seven original deadly sins, we all experience them emotionally: pride, covetousness, lust, anger, gluttony, envy and sloth.

Although we don't claim to be a theolgian, these emotions only become a sin when taken to excess. . . . The one we are adding to the list —greed—is usually associated with money matters. And, it can be a positive motivating factor.

It's greed, for example, that's one of the factors pushing a chief executive to build a successful company. But, in the following, we are using greed in sinful versions:

It's greed that prompts you to put all of your money in one stock.

It's greed when you act on a tip without knowing anything about the company.

It's greed that causes you to hastily accept information on a stock that does not come from a reliable source.

It's greed that encourages you to use money for investments that's earmarked for living expenses.

It's greed that causes you to put funds into a situation that "sounds too good to be true."

It's greed when you don't use our Selling Plan and sell half when a stock doubles.

It's greed when you do not diversify by buying 12 to 18 minipriced issues.

It's greed when you anguish over a booming stock you didn't buy.

WARRANTS:
A LANGUAGE OF THEIR OWN

There is a growing number of warrants being issued. And, they're providing a playground for those who like low-priced equities. For those who appreciate leverage. For those who can handle risk.

The warrant story is intertwined with the penny stock market. . . . There is a market subculture of people who formerly played penny stocks, who now find they can get similar leverage with warrants.

And, when we talk about penny stocks, we're talking about stocks that sell for less than $1—actually, in pennies.

While you currently find stocks selling for under $1 on the exchanges and Nasdaq, they are fallen angels— once priced much higher. Now there are no initial public offerings (IPOs) of stocks with price of 5¢, 25¢, 50¢, etc.

In the 1970s and much of the 1980s, there was a roaring market in penny issues, with much of the action centered in Denver. However, although there were many players who made good money legitimately buying and selling the pennies, that market was abused. There were many IPOs denominated in pennies. But, there was manipulation, by brokerage firms and individual brokers.

The regulators have effectively cleaned up that market. That's why there are no initial offerings in pennies. And, we believe that was a good effort.

Now, the stock of many smaller companies is being offered in units that are priced $5 or more a unit. And, a typical unit might consist of two shares of common and one warrant, with the latter thrown in as a "sweetener," to make the offering more attractive. Many buyers of the units believe they are getting the warrants for nothing. Too, shortly after the offering, with most units, the common and the warrants are uncoupled and begin trading separately. . . . As a consequence, we have a greater number of warrants coming onto the market.

Some investor are fearful of playing warrants, saying that they don't understand them. However, they are little different than common stocks. Both are quoted in stock tables. Certificates are issued for them, just as for any other type of stock. . . . But, warrants do have a language of their own. So, let's clear that up.

Definition

A warrant is simply an option issued by a corporation to buy a number of shares (usually one) of its common stock at a given price for a specified period of time. However, there are exceptions to that basic definition.

In case you're curious, common exceptions are warrants issued by one company for stock it owns in another company, warrants for partial or multiple shares of common or exerciseable into bonds or preferred stock. There can be various classes of warrants, with each expiring on a different date and with a different "exercise" price.

Exercise Price

This is the price at which the warrant holder can purchase the underlying stock. This is also referred to sometimes as the "strike price." . . . To illustrate, Nasdaq's Aid Auto Stores has a warrant that is selling for around 38¢ each. The exercise price is $4.00. This means that if you wanted to "exercise" the warrants, it would cost you $4.00 + 38¢ = $4.38. However, since the common is only selling for $2.59 as we write this, it would not be economical to make the conversion.

Intrinsic Value

This is the difference between the exercise and the stock price. If the stock is above the strike price, the warrant has intrinsic value and is said to be "in the money." With the stock below the strike price, the warrant has no intrinsic value (only time value) and is said to be "out of the money," as is illustrated with our Aid Auto Stores example in the above paragraph.

Call Feature

Increasingly, companies have insisted they have a right to "call" a warrant. They do this, because if they didn't, and both the common and warrants keep going up in price, there would be no incentive to convert the warrants. And, the firms want the cash that comes with conversion.

So, the company says they'll redeem the warrants when certain factors are met. Usually, they will pay a minimum amount. Again, let's look at Aid Auto Stores. The company says that if the common is 150% of the exercise price ($4.00 x 1.50 = $6.00) they will redeem the warrants. If you don't want to convert, they'll pay you 10¢ for each warrant.

Leverage

Once a stock begins moving up, one dollar invested in the company's warrants can do the work of several dollars invested in the common.

Why? Because as the stock approaches the price at which the warrants can be exercised, the price af the warrants, which sell for less than the stock, usually rises faster than the common. Thus, the investor can get a lot more action for less money.

Nevertheless, as always, leverage is good or bad. For example, the common of a well-known airline dropped from a high of 20⅞ to 17⅞ for a loss in value of only 14%. The warrants at the same time dropped from 16 to 9⅝ for a 40% decline.

History

Warrants have been around a long time. But, for much of that time they were treated as stepchildren in the investment family.

That perception was changed in April 1970 when the American Telephone & Telegraph Co. included them in a $1.57 million offering. And, their stature was further enhanced by the New York Stock Exchange, which made the AT&T warrants the first to be listed.

Company Rationale

Why do some companies like warrants? . . . At the beginning of this article, we explained how they are usually part of an initial public offering (and sometimes a secondary). . . . But, the big attraction is that they are an excellent vehicle for generating cash in the future. And, unlike a bank loan, this is "free" money in that it doesn't have to be paid back. Too, there isn't the obligation to make interest payments, as is true with any kind of debenture.

On the negative side, there is dilution when the warrants are exercised. However, experience has shown that if the resulting increase in shares is coupled with a hike in profits, there is no problem.

Tips On Playing Warrants

Many novices believe that when they buy a warrant, they have to hold it until the exercise price is reached and then they have to buy the common. But, that is not true. It is estimated that only about 20% of all warrants are exercised.

The warrants that we favor cost less than $1 to buy. In many cases the underlying stock can be in the $5 to

$10 range. It is an opportunity to participate in sharp stock appreciation without shelling out a lot of money.

Don't buy a warrant unless you like the underlying stock. This is just common sense. If the stock doesn't appreciate above the exercise price, your warrant will expire worthless. You don't want that.

Diversification is important. Try for at least 12 different ones, And put, if you can, an equal amount in each one. One successful warrant player only puts $1,500 in each warrant. But, the amount depends on your personal finances.

Diversification is also important in that if the company with the underlying stock is taken over by another company, the warrants of the acquiree become worthless.

Be willing to spend some time watching your warrant investments. You don't want to ignore them and suddenly find that the company has begun redeeming the warrants. And, only buy warrants on the New York and American Stock Exchanges and Nasdaq. Prices are quoted in *The Wall Street Journal*, *Barron's* and the Sunday edition of *The New York Times*. *Investor's Business Daily* only has skimpy coverage of these securities.

Finally, remember that good money can be made in warrants. Thousands are proving this each day. They are an inexpensive way of playing the stock market.

The Bowser Report

HISTORICAL REVIEW

1977 - 2000

HOW HAVE WE DONE SINCE 1977?

Cindy Bowser, associate publisher of *The Bowser Report*, and her very able assistants—Katie Hoffer and Thelma Cockes—have again brought us the Annual Historical Review. In it, she notes what happened to every stock we've recommended since 1977. And, it's downright exhausting when we remember how we fretted and sweated over every one of those 442 issues.

We proudly present Bowser's Honor Roll. In the box on the next page. Twelve stocks made the list. Each accumulated gains of 1,500% or more. . . . Also impressive—the thirty-two with gains of 500% to 1,500%.

One factor has been consistent in these Historical Reviews. There are more losing stocks. On the loss side, 239. The gainers number 205. (There is a discrepancy in the total number because a few issues were recommended twice.) From this, we learn two things: (1) These are not stocks you buy and hold. You have to use our Selling Plan. (2) You need to diversify. . . . While the gainers were outnumbered—my oh my!—how they did gain! *Add up all of the minuses and pluses—it comes to 83,619% on the plus side—up from 50,263% last year.*

More statistics: 47% of the stocks we have recommended are still in business. 27% are bankrupt, ceased trading, etc., and 26% have merged, been acquired or bought out.

BOWSER'S HONOR ROLL

The following recommendations,
as revealed by the new Historical Review,
had gains of 1,500% and over :

Stock	Mkt	Date Picked	Gain	
Semtech Corp	(O)	6/86	12,400%	
Smithfield Foods	(O)	7/77	5,483%	
Alpha Industries	(O)	6/77	4,833%	
MICROS Systems	(O)	11/91	4,580%	
Three-Five Sys	(N)	5/91	4,477%	
MICROS Systems	(O)	10/84	4,130%	
Continental Can	(N)	9/80	2,860%	(1)
MacAndrew/Forb	(N)	2/78	2,400%	(2)
Telex Corp	(N)	6/77	2,380%	(3)
Cognitronics	(A)	4/79	2,236%	
Sterling Elec	(A)	9/77	2,000%	(4)
Envirodyne	(O)	4/84	1,500%	(5)

(N) New York Stock Exchange; (A) American
Stock Exchange; (O) Nasdaq;
(1) Merged @ $37/share; (2) Went private @ $53.25/share;
(3) Merged @ $62/share; (4)Merged @ $21/share;
(5)Merged @ $40/share.

COLUMN HEADINGS

NAME: The name of the issue as first recommended or as it has emerged through name changes, etc. Next to it, we show the exchange it was on when originally recommended (i.e., OTC, NYSE, ASE). If it is still active and being traded, we show the current exchange and the symbol (O = Over the Counter, N = New York Stock Exchange, A = American Stock Exchange). If we can find no information whatsoever for the stock, we show (NI) next to the name. If the stock is now on the Pink Sheets, we show (OP) next to the name. (BB) denotes Nasdaq's Bulletin Board.

DATE-PRICE: This is the edition of *The Bowser Report* in which this stock was recommended as a Best Buy or Company of the Month. In early editions more than two Best Buys were frequently selected. However, during most of the newsletter's history, there were two Best Buys monthly. In Jan '88, the "Best Buy" designation was abandoned and we began having the "Company of the Month." OTC ask prices are used in this column.

CURRENT PRICE: This is the price of the stock as of February 18, 2000.

% GAIN/LOSS: The percentage of gain or loss from the time the stock became a Best Buy or Company of the Month until the price on February 18, 2000 or until it was merged, bought out, ceased trading, etc.

HIGH PRICE: The highest price reached by the stock following our recommendation up until February 18, 2000.

NAME	DATE - PRICE	CURRENT PRICE	% GAIN LOSS	HIGH PRICE	NOTES
ACTION PROD INT'L(O:APII)	1/96 - 1.94	2.94	+0052	6.44	
ACTRADE INT'L(O:ACRT)	06/93 - 2.31	16.50	+0614	30.00	
ADAMS DRUG(NYSE)	11/77 - 2.88	Merged @ 24.39	+0747	24.39	
ADAMS RESOURCES(A:AE)	12/84 - 4.00	11.00	+0175	18.38	Adjusted for 1-for-2 reverse 2/92
ADMAR GROUP(O:ADMR)	01/94 - 2.63	Merged @ 2.25	-0014	3.00	Merged with Principle Health Care 3/96
ADVANCE TECH PROD(O:ATPX)	7/78 - 1.75	8.75	+0400	15.00	Was Lunn Industries
AEGIS CORP(ASE)	5/81 - 2.63	Merged @ 6	+0128	6.00	
AERO SVCS INT(BB:BFST)	1/84 - 2.63	0.40	-0092	4.13	
AERO SYSTEMS(O:AERS)	8/78 - 2.38	1.94	-0018	9.38	
AERONCA INC(ASE)	7/82 - 2.75	Merged @ 6	+0118	6.00	Merged with Fleet Aerospace Corp in Jun '86.
AEROSONIC(A:AIM)	12/81 - 2.63	11.00	+0318	16.25	
AEROTRON(OTC)	8/77 - 2.50	Merged @ 8	+0220	8.00	
AFP IMAGING(BB:AFPC)	10/84 - 2.88	0.56	-0081	4.00	
AILEEN(NYSE)	8/79 - 2.38	0.00	-0100	21.88	Bankrupt
AIM TELEPHONE(ASE)	12/84 - 2.75	0.00	-0100	12.50	Bankrupt
AIR METHODS(O:AIRM)	10/99 - 2.69	4.25	+0058	4.25	
AJAY SPORTS(BB:AJAY)	5/92 - 1.50	1.00	-0033	1.66	
ALBA - WALDEN(A:AWS)	11/77 - 2.13	18.25	+0757	28.88	
ALLIED DEVICES(O:ALDV)	2/97 - 2.50	2.94	+0018	2.96	
ALLOU HEALTH(A:ALU)	10/90 - 1.88	7.81	+0315	10.63	
ALLSTAR SYSTEMS(O:ALLS)	1/00 - 1.75	2.94	+0068	3.56	
ALPHA IND(O:AHAA)	6/77 - 2.63	129.75	+4833	129.75	
ALPHA MICROSYS(O:ALMI)	See Alpha Serv.com				
ALPHAREL INC(O:AREL)	See Altris Software				
ALPHASERV.COM(O:ALMI)	1/93 - 2.25	6.88	+0206	6.94	Was Alpha Microsystems
ALPINE INT'L(NI)	12/80 - 2.63	0.00	-0100	3.00	Ceased trading
ALTEC CORP(NI)	12/78 - 1.00	0.00	-0100	1.50	Ceased trading
ALTERNATE MKTG(O:ALTM)	12/99 - 2.06	2.41	+0017	2.63	
ALTRIS SOFTWARE(BB:ALTS)	9/91 - 4.38	3.38	+0023	9.75	Was Alpharel Inc. 1-for-2 reverse 10/96
AMATI COMM(O:AMTX)	2/80 - 2.63	Buyout @ 20.00	+0660	36.50	Was Microfoam Data, then ICOT Corp.; Acquired by Texas Instru Mar '98.
AMBAS FOOD SVCS(BB:AMBF)	4/84 - 2.63	0.28	-0089	3.38	Was Automatique
AMER AGRON(NYSE)	See Orange Corp.				

NAME	DATE - PRICE	CURRENT PRICE	% GAIN LOSS	HIGH PRICE	NOTES
AMER ED PROD(O:AMEP)	7/91 - 7.50	10.00	+0033	12.31	1-for-5 reverse Apr '97
AMER FIRST CORP(OTC)	7/87 - 2.25	0.00	-0100	3.00	Bankrupt
AMER FUEL TECH(NI)	5/83 - 2.38	0.00	-0100	4.69	Ceased trading
AMER MED ALERT(O:AMAC)	4/92 - 2.25	3.25	+0044	4.44	
AMER MIDLAND(OP)	2/82 - 0.94	0.00	-0100	1.56	No Market. Was Midland Resource.
AMER NAT'L EN(OTC)	10/85 - 1.94	Merged @ 1.51	-0022	3.50	Merged with Peregrine Entertainment Nov '86.
AMER OIL & GAS(NYSE)	12/81 - 8.25	Buyout at 11.63	+0041	16.13	Restated 1-for-4 reverse split May '82; acquired by KN Energy 7/94.
AMER PHYSICIAN(O:AMPH)	1/87 - 2.81	3.75	+0033	8.25	
AMER PLAN(ASE)	9/79 - 2.13	0.00	-0100	8.63	Liquidated
AMER SPORTS ADV(NI)	1/82 - 18.10	0.00	-0100	2.50	1-for-10 reverse split, Jan '90. Ceased trading.
AMER SURG CTRS(OP)	4/82 - 2.13	0.00	-0100	18.50	Bankrupt
AMER VISION(NI)	12/80 - 2.06	0.00	-0100	3.50	Ceased trading
AMREP(N:AXR)	1/78 - 1.06	5.25	+0395	23.88	Restated 5-for-4 split Nov '84 & 3-for-2 Dec '86.
ANALYTICAL SUR(O:ANLT)	2/89 - 2.75	8.00	+0191	47.25	
ANIMED INC(OP)	11/87 - 2.13	0.00	-0100	4.38	Bankrupt
ANNANDALE CORP(NI)	3/83 - 2.13	0.00	-0100	3.88	Ceased trading
APOLLO IND(OTC)	10/83 - 2.00	Merged @ 1.65	-0018	3.00	Merged Dec '87 with J. L. Can Inc. @ $1.65.
APOLLO LASERS(OTC)	12/78 - 2.75	Merged @ 8.50	+0209	8.63	
APPOINT TECH(OP)	9/85 - 0.75	0.00	-0100	3.25	Was Standard Logic. Ceased trading
ARIS IND(BB:ALSI)	1/79 - 1.75	1.88	+0007	7.63	Was Marcade Group. 1-for-5 rev 2/99.
ARIZONA INSTRU(O:AZIC)	9/95 - 8.75	Acquired at 5.00	-0043	5.00	1-for-5 rev 2/99. Acquired by CEO @ $5/share 2/00.
ARMATRON INT(OP:ATRM)	12/79 - 2.75	0.13	-0095	17.75	
ART EXPLOSION(OTC)	6/84 - 2.31	Merged @ .39	-0098	4.38	Merged with Decor Corp. Mar '86 @ $0.39.
ARTISTIC GREETGS(O:ARTG)	11/86 - 2.75	Buyout @ 5.70	+0107	11.50	Acquired by MDC Communications May '98
ASPEN IMAGING(OP)	2/86 - 2.63	Acquired @ 1.18	-0055	5.00	Acquired by Pubco Corp. 6/96; 1 Pubco share for every 7 Aspen shares
ASPEN RIBBONS(OTC)	See Aspen Imaging				

NAME	DATE - PRICE	CURRENT PRICE	% GAIN LOSS	HIGH PRICE	NOTES
ATI INC(ASE)	9/79 - 2.75	0.00	-0100	6.13	Bankrupt
ATLANTIC MET(NYSE)	See Hallwood Group.				
AUDIOTRONICS(OP)	11/86 - 2.38	0.00	-0100	3.13	No Market
AULT INC(O:AULT)	1/92 - 2.56	9.50	+0271	16.50	
AUTOINFO(BB:AUTO)	12/88 - 1.63	0.17	-0090	5.63	
AUTOMATIQUE(OTC)	See Ambas Food Srvs				
AUTOMOBILE PROT (O:APCO)	3/94 - 2.34	Acqd @ 13.00	+0456	14.94	Acquired by Ford Motor Co. 7/99.
AVALON CORP(OP)	11/79 - 3.00	Merged @ 7.81	+0025	7.50	Merged w. Dundee Bancorp. 2/93. Was Tri-South Ind.
AVALON CORR SERV(O:CITY)	4/99 - 2.63	1.81	-0031	3.13	
AZTEC TECH PART(O:AZTC)	11/99 - 1.38	6.78	+0391	6.79	
BANCINSURANCE(O:BCIS)	7/92 - 1.88	5.25	+0179	7.50	
BARCO OF CALIF(ASE)	3/81 - 2.75	Buyout @ 5.05	+0084	7.63	Leveraged buyout by company 10/87 @ $5.05.
BASIC RESOUR(OTC)	See Basix Corp.				
BASIX CORP(OP)	6/78 - 2.13	0.00	-0100	13.88	No Market. Was Basic Resource.
BCT INT'L(O:BCTI)	1/99 - 2.81	1.94	-0031	3.13	
BFC FINANCIAL (BB:BFCFA)	2/83 - 2.88	3.19	+0007	48.00	1-for-3 rev 3/86 1-for-2 rev 1/89 3-for-1 2/98. Was IRE Financial
BFX HOSPITAL GRP(A:BFX)	9/83 - 6.40	0.94	-0085	9.13	1-for-5 reverse 10/85. Was Buffton Corp.
BICKFORD CORP(ASE)	7/77 - 2.13	Merged @ 2.25	+0006	3.00	
BIO-DENTAL TECH(O:BDTC)	12/92 - 2.25	Merged @ 5.78	+0157	6.69	Merged with Zila Inc.
BIOPOOL INT'L(BB:BIPL)	02/93 - 2.50	1.00	-0060	3.81	
BIRTCHER(OP)	12/77 - 2.00	Merged @ 19.00	+0850	19.25	Merged with Conmed Mar '95 @ 19
BISCAYNE APPAREL(OP)	12/87 - 2.88	0.00	-0100	5.00	Was Biscayne Holdings. No Market
BISCAYNE HOLDINGS(ASE)	See Biscayne Apparel				
BISHOP GRAPHIC(OTC)	See Bishop Inc				
BISHOP INC(OP)	3/79 - 3.00	0.00	-0100	10.25	No Market. Was Bishop Graphic.
BOMAINE CORP(OTC)	8/79 - 2.25	Buyout @ 11	+0389	11.00	Leveraged buyout by management Sep '84.
BRADLEY PHARM(O:BPRX)	6/98 - 2.19	2.41	+0010	2.41	

NAME	DATE - PRICE	CURRENT PRICE	% GAIN LOSS	HIGH PRICE	NOTES
BRIGADIER IND(ASE)	4/79 - 2.75	Merged @ 3.98	+0045	3.98	Merged in stock swap with U.S. Home in 1982.
BRT REALTY(N:BRT)	6/85 - 8.25	8.06	-0002	19.38	Restated 1-for-3 reverse split Aug '86; began trading NYSE Jan '88.
BUCKHORN INC(ASE)	2/85 - 2.75	Buyout @ 5.38	+0096	5.38	Bought by Myers Industries @ $5.38 6/87.
BUFFTON CORP(A:BFX)	See BFX Hospital Group				
BULL & BEAR(O:BNBGA)	See Winmill & Co.				
BURTON HAWKS(OTC)	See Hawks Indus				Reorganized 12/88 as Hawks Ind., basis: 1 Hawks Ind for each common.
CABLE CAR BEV(O:DRNK)	7/94 - 0.94	Merged @ 4.11	+0337	4.11	Merged with Triarc Co. @ 4.11 11/97.
CABOT MEDICAL(OTC)	6/86 - 2.00	Merged @ 9.08	+0354	20.13	Merged with Circon Corp. Apr '95
CACHE INC(O:CACH)	4/83 - 11.50	3.94	-0066	11.50	Restated 1-for-4 reverse split Sep '93
CAMPBELL RES(N:CCH)	9/87 - 2.50	0.28	-0089	2.75	
CANNON PICTURES(OP)	8/83 - 2.00	0.00	-0100	3.38	Was Twenty-First Century. No Market
CANTERBURY CORP(O:XCEL)	See Canterbury InfoTech				
CANTERBURY ED(OTC)	See Canterbury Corp				
CANTERBURY INFO (O:CITI)	11/92 - 7.89	4.12	-0048	6.25	Was Canterbury Corp. 1-for-3 rev 4/98.
CARDIFF COMMUN(OTC)	1/83 - 1.00	Liquitd @ 2.38	+0069	2.44	Liquidated 12/86 @ 2.38/share.
CARDIFF EQUITIES(ASE)	4/78 - 2.00	Merged @ 12.84	+0542	12.84	Merged w. Leucadia Nat'l Corp 1/86; was TFI Companies.
CARDINAL IND(OP)	1/87 - 1.81	0.00	-0100	2.69	Bankrupt
CARME INC(OTC)	5/84 - 7.12	Bought @ 5.25	-0026	11.75	1-for-3 rev 8/86. Bot 1/90 by Int'l Res & Dev Corp.
CASCADE INT'L(NI)	12/89 - 2.88	0.00	-0100	11.75	Liquidated
CBL MEDICAL(OP)	1/91 - 2.75	0.00	-0100	8.38	Bankrupt
CELLU-CRAFT(ASE)	9/78 - 3.00	Merged @ 9	+0200	10.63	Private group acquisition Mar '84 @ $9.00.
CENCOR(BB:CCOO)	10/77 - 0.66	0.00	-0100	17.50	3-for-1 split Apr '85 3-for-2 Apr '86 1-for-5 Aug '90. Sold assets.
CENTRONICS(NYSE)	See EKCO Group.				
CERTRON CORP(BB:CTRN)	3/80 - 1.00	0.51	-0049	4.50	

NAME	DATE - PRICE	CURRENT PRICE	% GAIN LOSS	HIGH PRICE	NOTES
CHAMPION ENTER(A:CHB)	8/81 - 13.15	7.38	-0044	40.63	1-for-5 rev Jun '87. Was Champion Home.
CHAMPION HOME(ASE)	See Champion Enterprises.				
CHEM INT'L(O:CXIL)	8/98 - 2.50	2.12	-0015	2.88	
CHINA RESOURCES(O:CHRB)	4/97 - 27.50	9.00	-0067	13.13	1-for-10 rev 6/99.
CHIPWICH INC(NI)	3/90 - 0.81	0.00	-0100	1.44	Ceased trading
CIRCLE FINE ART(OP)	3/87 - 3.00	0.00	-0100	10.75	No Market
CMS ADVERTISING(OTC)	See UNICO				
COBRA ELECTRONICS(O:COBR)	11/96 - 2.50	5.94	+0178	10.87	
COGENIC ENERGY(OTC)	11/82 - 2.81	0.00	-0100	8.25	Bankrupt
COGNITRONICS(A:CGN)	4/79 - 0.95	22.19	+2236	24.38	Restated 3-for-2 split '92. 3-for-2 spLit 8/99.
COLLINS IND(O:COLL)	3/88 - 2.50	5.81	+0112	8.75	
COLORADO MEDTECH(O:CMED)	3/86 - 4.70	12.38	+0163	14.75	1-for-10 rev 3/90. Was Cybermedics.
COMMAND SECURITY(O:CMMD)	7/96 - 1.50	1.12	-0025	2.84	
COMMER DECAL(NI)	9/78 - 1.63	0.00	-0100	8.00	Bankrupt
COMMODORE COR(ASE)	10/79 - 2.63	0.00	-0100	13.38	Bankrupt
COMPUTER IDENTICS(O:CIDN)	11/91 - 1.44	Merged @ 2.73	+0090	3.13	Merged with Robotic Visions
COMTECH TELECOMM(O:CMTL)	1/97 - 2.75	17.56	+0539	25.63	3-for-2 split 8/99.
CONOLOG CORP(O:CNLG)	6/84 - 1.42	5.19	+0265	9.25	
CONQUEST AIRLINES(OP)	See ConquestIndustries				
CONQUEST IND(NI)	08/93 - 24.10	0.00	-0100	3.88	1-for-10 rev 11/94. Was Conquest Airlines.
CONSOLIDATED MER(O:CSLMF)	6/96 - 3.94	1.25	-0068	2.75	1-for-2 rev.10/98.
CONSUL RESTAU(OP)	11/85 - 2.00	0.00	-0100	4.38	Bankrupt
CONTINENTAL CAN(N:CAN)	9/80 - 1.25	Merged @ 37.00	+2860	41.06	2-for-1 10/87. Was Viatech. Merged with Suiza Foods 6/98.
COOK UNITED(NI)	2/78 - 3.00	0.00	-0100	10.38	Bankrupt
COSMETIC GROUP(NI)	SeeZegarelli Group				
COSMOPOL CARE(ASE)	12/87 - 1.25	Merged @ 4.04	+0223	4.04	Merger with Norrell Corp @ $4.04 Oct '88.
COSMOPOL CARE(OTC)	1/85 - 2.88	Merged @ 4.04	+0040	4.04	See above
CREATIVE COMP (A:CAP.EC)	1/95 - 2.88	2.62	-0009	3.13	
CREDO PETROL(O:CRED)	12/80 - 14.38	3.31	-0077	3.69	Restated 1-for-10 reverse split Oct '82.
CREST-FOAM(ASE)	4/80 - 2.75	Merged @ 14.50	+0408	16.63	Acquired by L&P Foam Feb '87 @ $14.50.

✦ HISTORICAL REVIEW ✦

NAME	DATE - PRICE	CURRENT PRICE	% GAIN LOSS	HIGH PRICE	NOTES
CRITICARE SYS(O:CXIM)	2/91 - 2.88	2.44	+0015	9.00	
CSM ENVIRON(BB:CSMY)	4/86 - 250.00	10.00	-0096	150	Adjusted 1-for-100 reverse 1996. Was CSM Systems.
CSM SYSTEMS(OTC)	See CSMEnvironmental				
CYBERMEDIC INC(NI)	See Colorado MedTech				
CZECH IND(NI)	See Eastbrokers				
DASH INDUS(NI)	See David & Dash				
DATA TREND SYS(O:DATA)	9/88 - 1.13	6.09	+0439	6.09	Was Star Classics, then Starmark and Babystar
DATATRON INC(OTC)	12/83 - 2.13	0.00	-0100	3.00	Bankrupt
DATAWATCH CORP(O:DWCH)	5/95 - 2.69	4.88	+0081	11.63	
DATUM INC(O:DATM)	8/80 - 2.38	15.44	+0549	24.50	
DAVID & DASH(NI)	8/83 - 1.19	0.00	-0100	1.19	Was Dash Industries
DE ROSE IND(ASE)	8/80 - 2.00	0.00	-0100	12.13	Bankrupt
DECORATOR IND(A:DII)	6/81 - 1.50	5.12	+0241	18.88	1-for-2 rev 7/82
					3-for-2 split 12/84.
DELTA DATA(OTC)	11/83 - 2.75	0.00	-0100	3.38	Bankrupt
DESIGNCRAFT IND(NI)	8/77 - 1.70	0.00	-0100	15.38	10% stock div 9/87. Was Designcraft Jewels.
DESIGNCRAFT JWLS(ASE)	See Designcraft Industries.				
DETROIT-TX GAS(NI)	7/84 - 2.56	0.00	-0100	3.00	Ceased trading
DIAGNOSTIC HEALTH(BB:DHSM	10/94 - 1.94	0.25	-0087	15.25	
DIAN CONTROLS(NI)	3/85 - 2.63	0.00	-0100	3.50	Ceased trading
DISCOUNT FAB(ASE)	3/79 - 1.75	Merged @ 3.25	+0086	3.25	
DIVERSIFAX INC(OP:DFAX)	5/94 - 2.53	0.01	-0100	13.00	
DIVERSIFIED IND(OP)	See EZConnect				
DREW INDUSTRIES(A:DW)	3/82 - 8.10	8.62	+0006	27.25	Adjusted for 1-for-10 reverse split 5/89
DREXLER TEC(O:DRXR)	6/77 - 3.00	10.00	+0233	24.00	
DURATEK CORP(OTC)	See GTS Duratek				
DXP ENTERPRISES(O:DXPE)	8/85 - 2.88	2.62	-0009	11.00	Was Newman Communications, then Index, Inc.
DYANSEN CORP(NI)	9/86 - 1.75	0.00	-0100	5.25	Ceased trading. Was Fine Art Acq.
DYNA GROUP INT'L(BB:DGIX)	12/93 - 0.94	0.51	-0046	1.38	
DYNATEC INT'L(O:DYNX)	10/85 - 5.60	1.44	-0074	7.75	Restated for 1-for-10 reverse split, Jul '90.
DYNATRONICS(O:DYNT)	3/98 - 1.00	1.44	+0044	5.88	

NAME	DATE - PRICE	CURRENT PRICE	% GAIN LOSS	HIGH PRICE	NOTES
EA INDUSTRIES(OP:EAIN)	12/77 - 2.63	0.03	-0099	16.38	Was Electronic Associates.
EAGLE TELEPHON(OP)	7/86 - 2.63	0.00	-0100	4.00	Bankrupt
EARLY CALIF IND(OTC)	See ERLY Industries.				
EASTBROKERS INT'L(O:EAST)	See Global Capital Partners				
EATERIES INC(O:EATS)	2/92 - 1.56	3.00	+0092	6.13	
EDMOS CORP(NI)	4/79 - 2.63	0.00	-0100	2.63	Ceased trading
EDUC DEV CORP(O:EDUC)	8/92 - 1.06	3.50	+0230	26.25	Adjusted for 2-for-1 split Apr '96.
EFI ELEC CORP(BB:EFIC)	11/90 - 2.81	1.19	-0058	6.63	
EGAMES INC(O:EGAM)	5/98 - 2.41	4.00	+0066	5.06	Was Romtech Inc.
EKCO GROUP(N:EKO)	2/88 - 2.13	Acquired @ 7.00	+0229	14.00	Acquired by Corning Consumer Prod. @ $7 8/99. Was Centronics.
ELEC ASSOC(NYSE)	See E.A. Industries				
ELSINORE CORP(BB:ELSO)	11/87 - 10.00	4.00	-0060	8.38	Adjusted for 1-for-5 reverse 7/91.
EMCOR PETROL(OTC)	10/80 - 2.38	Merged @ 6.50	+0173	7.50	Merged Sep '85 into Energy Development Partners.
EMPIRE GOLD(NI)	3/78 - 3.00	0.00	-0100	11.00	Was National Enterprises. Ceased trading
ENGINEER MEAS(O:EMCO)	7/82 - 2.20	7.38	+0235	12.75	5-for-4 split 11/98.
ENVIRODYNE IND(OTC)	4/84 - 2.50	Merged @ 40	+1500	40.00	Merged @ $40.00 Mar '89.
ENVIROGEN(O:ENVG)	9/97 - 16.50	4.19	-0075	4.56	1-for-6 rev 11/98
ERLY IND(OP)	6/77 - 2.77	0.00	-0100	17.75	10% stock div 9/90. Was Early Calif. Ind.
ESPRIT SYSTEMS(OTC)	5/86 - 1.75	Acquired @ .17	-0090	2.75	Acquired 7/90 @ $.17 by Taiwanese group.
ET BARWICK IND(NI)	5/79 - 2.00	0.00	-0100	2.00	Ceased trading
EVERGREEN HEALTHCAR(NYSE)	3/92 - 3.13	Merged @ 13.37	+0327	13.37	Adj for 1-for-5 rev Jun '93. Was Nat'l Heritage. Merged w. Grancare.
EZCONNECT(BB:EZCT)	2/79 - 2.75	7.37	+0168	8.75	Was Diversified Industries
FABRI-TEK INC(OTC)	2/81 - 2.88	Merged @ 6	+0108	6.13	
FAMOUS RESTAUR(OP)	8/86 - 2.06	0.00	-0100	4.13	No Market
FASTCOMM COMM(BB:FSCX)	10/91 - 2.75	4.84	+0076	12.63	
FIFTH AVE CARD(OTC)	See Fifth Retail.				
FIFTH RETAIL(NI)	4/83 - 2.13	0.00	-0100	4.38	Ceased trading. Was Fifth Ave Card.
FIND/SVP INC(O:FSVP)	6/89 - 2.25	3.88	+0072	3.88	
FINE ART ACQ(OTC)	See DyansenCorporation.				

NAME	DATE - PRICE	CURRENT PRICE	% GAIN LOSS	HIGH PRICE	NOTES
FIRECOM INC(BB:FRCM)	9/86 - 1.19	0.70	-0041	1.38	
FIRETECTOR INC(O:FTEC)	10/95 - 3.39	2.88	-0015	3.38	1-for-3 reverse split Sep '98
FLORAFAX INT(BB:FIIF)	1/78 - 2.25	Merged @ 15.21	+0576	21.88	Merged with Gerald Stevens 5/99
FLORIDA CAP(ASE)	3/80 - 2.75	Merged @ 21	+0664	21.00	
FOCUS ENHANCEMENT(O:FCSE)	8/97 - 2.47	6.56	+0166	7.50	
FRANKLIN CON(O:FKCM)	See WCM Capital Inc.				
FROST & SULLIV(OTC)	6/79 - 2.25	Merged @ 10	+0344	10.13	Jan 26'88 merged with FAS Acquisition Co.
GALVESTON-HOUS(OP)	4/89 - 3.00	Merged @ 2.25	-0025	6.88	Merged with GHX Acquisition Feb '95 @ 2.25.
GAYNOR-STAFF(ASE)	10/78 - 2.25	Merged @ .20	-0091	2.25	Merged with New Merger Corp. Jun '85 @ $0.20.
GEMCO NATIONAL(ASE)	See Investor Ins Grp				
GEN HOUSEWARES(N:GHW)	7/77 - 3.00	Acqrd @ 28.75	+0858	29.75	Acquired by Borden's @ 28.75
GENERAL DEVICES(OP)	9/84 - 1.88	0.00	-0100	2.88	No Market
GENTNER COMM(O:GTNR)	2/98 - 1.22	14.62	+1098	15.88	
GEO INT'L(NI)	9/90 - 2.63	0.00	-0100	2.63	Ceased trading
GEODYNE RESOUR(ASE)	10/89 - 3.00	Merged @ 1.22	-0059	3.25	Merged with Samson Investment
GEOTEL INC(OP)	10/82 - 1.88	0.00	-0100	4.38	No Market
GI EXPORT(ASE)	See Johnston Industries				
GLOBAL CAPITAL(O:GCAP)	8/96 - 7.80	9.75	+0025	11.25	1-for-5 rev 9/96. Was Eastbrokers International.
GLOBESAT HOLDING(NI)	8/84 - 0.88	0.00	-0100	0.88	Ceased trading. Was Questronics.
GO-VIDEO INC(A:VCR)	See Sensory Science Corp.				
GOLDEN EAGLE GRP(O:GEGP)	3/96 - 2.44	Merged @ 4.45	+0082	4.93	Merged with U.S. Freightways
GOLDEN GENESIS(O:GGGO)	8/95 - 1.81	Acquired @ 2.33	+0029	3.38	Acquired by Kyocera Int'l @ 2.33 8/99.
					Was Photocomm.
GRAND ADV TOUR(O:GATT)	9/99 - 2.69	6.00	+0123	6.25	
GRAND TOYS INT'L(O:GRIN)	12/96 - 6.55	4.44	-0032	8.37	Adjusted 1-for-5 reverse Aug '95
GREENMAN BROS(ASE)	See Noodle Kadoodle				
GREG MANNING AUC(O:GMAI)	8/94 - 2.88	19.38	+0573	24.13	
GRIFFON CORP(A:GFF)	1/84 - 3.00	8.12	+0171	17.50	Was Instrument Systems.

NAME	DATE - PRICE	CURRENT PRICE	% GAIN LOSS	HIGH PRICE	NOTES
GROLIER INC(NYSE)	3/81 - 2.06	Merged @ 21	+0919	21.00	Merged Apr '88 with Hachette S.A. @ $21.00.
GTI CORP(O:GGTI)	8/79 - 1.75	Buyout @ 3.10	+0077	33.75	Acquired by Technitrol Inc. Nov '98
GTS DURATEK(O:DRTK)	11/87 - 2.75	8.00	+0191	17.87	Was Duratek Corp.
GULL LABS(A:GUL)	8/91 - 2.81	Buyout @ 2.25	-0020	12.50	Acquired by Meridian Diagnostics Nov '98
HADRON INC(BB:HDRN)	3/82 - 2.25	0.66	-0071	4.13	
HALLWOOD GROUP(N:HWG)	6/82 - 0.75	10.69	+1325	40.75	Was Atlantic Met. & UMET Property, 3-for-2 10/99.
HALSEY DRUG(A:HDG)	3/87 - 2.00	2.25	+0013	11.31	Adjusted for two 5% stock dividends.
HARVEY ELECT(O:HRVE)	8/85 - 1.38	1.50	+0009	3.75	Was Harvey Group
HARVEY ELECT(O:HRVE)	2/79 - 2.75	1.50	-0045	9.50	Was Harvey Group
HARVEY GROUP(OTC)	See Harvey Electronics				
HAWKS IND(O:HAWK)	2/79 - 22.60	1.62	-0093	9.00	Was Burton Hawks. 1-for-20 rev 2/98.
HEALTH MGT(O:HMIS)	12/91 - 4.00	Merged @ 0.30	-0093	20.00	1-for-3 rev 3/92 3-for-2 12/95. Merged w. Transworld Healthcare
HEALTHTECH INT'L(O:GYMM)	7/97 - 1.34	0.00	-0100	2.43	Trading suspended
HEI INC(O:HEII)	8/88 - 3.00	10.00	+0233	12.38	
HELDOR IND(NI)	10/86 - 2.25	0.00	-0100	4.63	Ceased trading
HELM CAPITAL GRP(BB:HCGI)	4/82 - 2.00	0.38	-0081	4.50	Was Helm Resources
HELM RESOURCE(A:HHH)	See Helm Capital Group				
HEMACARE CORP(BB:HGMA)	11/88 - 2.50	2.94	+0018	12.13	
HEMDALE COMM(NI)	02/94 - 2.53	0.00	-0100	3.00	Ceased trading
HI-RISE RECYCL(O:HIRI)	11/98 - 2.06	2.44	+0018	4.06	
HLH PETROLEUM(OTC)	11/80 - 8.44	0.00	-0100	8.44	1-for-3 rev 11/80. Ceased operations.
HOAN PRODUCTS(NI)	5/82 - 1.18	0.00	-0100	3.63	2-for-1 split 6/83. Ceased trading.
HOFMANN IND(ASE)	6/77 - 3.00	Tender @ 8.25	+0175	8.25	Semi-private tender offer 1/90. Bot 91% of shares.
HOLIDAY RV SUPER(O:RVEE)	10/93 - 2.00	5.19	+0160	6.50	
HOMECARE MGMT(OTC)	See Health Management				
HORIZONS RESCH(OTC)	12/84 - 2.63	Acquired @ 4	+0052	7.13	Acquired by investor grp 2/88 @ $4.00.
HOSPITAL STAFF(OP)	4/87 - 2.63	0.00	-0100	16.63	Bankrupt
HOWARD B WOLF(A:HBW)	9/80 - 2.63	4.00	+0052	9.88	Dissolved @ $4.00 9/99.

NAME	DATE - PRICE	CURRENT PRICE	% GAIN LOSS	HIGH PRICE	NOTES
HYCOR BIOMEDICAL(O:HYBD)	8/87 - 1.63	3.88	+0138	8.63	
HYTEK INT'L(NI)	6/83 - 2.25	0.00	-0100	4.13	Ceased trading
IBI SECURITY(NI)	11/84 - 2.81	0.00	-0100	3.44	Ceased trading
IFS INT'L(O:IFSH)	7/99 - 2.50	4.62	+0085	5.69	
ILX INC(O:ILEX)	See ILX Resorts Inc.				
ILX RESORTS INC(A:ILX)	6/94 - 8.75	1.81	-0079	9.38	1-for-5 rev 1/98. Was ILX Inc.
IMPERIAL GROUP(ASE)	5/85 - 2.25	Merged @ 4.91	+0118	4.91	Acquired by Hanson Trust.
IMPERIAL IND(OP)	5/84 - 2.13	0.00	-0100	3.25	No Market
IN HOME HEALTH(O:IHHI)	1/90 - 5.82	2.31	-0060	7.00	1-for-3 rev.11/98.
INAMED CORP(O:IMDC)	9/89 - 2.75	35.88	+1205	47.13	
INDEX INC(OTC)	See DXP Enterprises				
INFLIGHT SVCS(NI)	2/80 - 2.25	0.00	-0100	12.63	Ceased trading
INSTRUMENT SYS(ASE)	See Griffon Corp.				
INT'L BANKNOTE(ASE)	1/80 - 2.88	Merged @ 3.12	+0008	10.38	Merged with U.S. Banknote JuL '90 for $3.12/share.
INT'L ELECTRONICS(O:IEIB)	9/96 - 2.00	3.06	+0053	3.06	
INT'L FD SVC(ASE)	10/77 - 1.75	Merged @ .96	-0045	3.00	
INT'L ROY OIL(OTC)	See Signature Motors				
INT'L STRETCH(NI)	5/79 - 1.00	0.00	-0100	1.38	Bankrupt
INTEGRAMED AMER(O:INMD)	4/95 - 6.52	3.06	-0053	6.28	1-for-4 reverse Nov '98. Was IVF America
INTEK DIVER(O:IDCC)	See Intek Global Corp.				
INTEK GLOBAL(O:IGLC)	3/81 - 2.94	Acquired @ 3.01	+0002	12.25	Acquired by IGC Acquisition @ 3.01 7/99. Was Intek Diversified
INTER PARFUMS(O:IPAR)	5/89 - 1.32	10.38	+0686	15.63	1-for-2.5 rev 8/90, 3-for-2 split 12/92. Was Jean Philippe Frag.
INTERM'T LABS(OTC)	8/82 - 1.41	Merged @ .47	-0067	5.13	Restated 3-for-2 split Aug '83; merged w/Cardio Petro Jun '85 @ $0.47.
INVESTORS INS GRP(BB:IIGI)	5/82 - 3.00	0.13	-0096	7.00	Was Gemco National
ION NETWORKS(O:IONN)	4/98 - 2.75	36.38	+1223	42.63	Was MicroFrame Inc.
IRE FINANCIAL(OTC)	See BFC Financial.				
ITEX CORP(OP:ITEX)	3/95 - 2.94	1.55	-0047	12.50	
IVF AMERICA(O:IVFA)	See Integramed Amer				
JANUS HOTELS(O:JAGI)	2/00 - 2.13	3.47	+0063	3.94	
JEAN PHILIPPE(O:JEAN)	See Inter Parfums				

NAME	DATE - PRICE	CURRENT PRICE	% GAIN LOSS	HIGH PRICE	NOTES
JEC LASERS(OP)	5/85 - 2.63	0.00	-0100	4.38	No Market
JETRONIC IND(A:JET)	10/79 - 2.38	1.06	-0055	10.00	
JEWELCOR(NYSE)	6/79 - 2.00	Bought @ 19	+0850	20.38	3-for-2 split 9/86; bought out 5/88 by Holtzman Grp @ 19
JILLIAN'S ENTER(O:QBAL)	5/87 - 6.24	0.00	-0100	1.56	1-for-4 rev 4/90. Was Metalbanc.
JIM HJELM PRIV(O:JHPC)	See JLM Couture				
JLM COUTURE(O:JHPC)	9/93 - 1.88	3.00	+0060	6.63	1-for-3 rev 1/95. Was Jim Hjelms.
JMAR INDUSTRIES(O:JMAR)	6/97 - 2.72	9.50	+0249	9.50	
JOHNSON PRODUCTS(A:JPC)	11/87 - 2.88	Merged @ 24.12	+0738	25.75	Merged with IVAX Corp Aug '93 @ 24.12.
JOHNSTON IND(N:JII)	9/78 - 2.00	1.88	-0006	16.88	Declared special year-end $0.50 dividend, payable Dec 5'88. Was GI Expt
JORDAN AMER HLDGS(BB:JAHI)	4/94 - 2.25	0.28	-0088	2.50	
KALVAR CORP(OTC)	9/80 - 3.00	Merged @ 2.70	-0010	3.25	Merged Oct '87 with MTech Corp. @ $2.70.
KAPLAN INDUS(OP)	10/83 - 1.75	0.00	-0100	3.00	No Market
KAY LABS(OTC)	9/81 - 2.13	Merged @ 1.83	-0014	2.69	
KDI CORP(NYSE)	7/79 - 2.94	Merged @ 19	+0546	19.63	Merged Nov '88 with KD Acquisition @ $19.00.
KIN-ARK(A:KIN)	8/77 - 2.50	1.75	-0030	10.63	
KLEER-VU IND(OP:KLVU)	11/78 - 1.70	0.01	-0099	12.75	Adjusted for stock dividends & stock splits.
KMS INDUSTRIES(OP)	1/83 - 22.00	0.00	-0100	13.00	Restated 1-for-8 reverse split Jun '87. No Market
KRANTOR CORP(O:KRAN)	See Synergy Brands				
LA POINTE IND(NI)	2/82 - 2.75	0.00	-0100	8.75	Bankrupt
LABARGE INC(A:LB)	7/95 - 2.50	2.94	+0018	10.88	
LANE WOOD(NI)	4/78 - 52.50	0.00	-0100	52.50	1-for-20 rev 11/86. Ceased trading
LEE PHARMACEU(BB:LPHM)	11/84 - 1.50	0.25	-0083	19.31	Restated 2-for-1 stock split Oct '86.
LEHIGH VALLEY(NYSE)	See LVI Group.				
LEISURE TECH(NI)	10/81 - 3.00	0.00	-0100	9.88	Ceased trading
LEXICON RES(OP)	2/81 - 1.75	0.00	- 0100	2.38	No Market
LLC CORP(NYSE)	See Valhi Incorporated.				
LLOYD'S ELECT(ASE)	1/82 - 0.75	Merged @ 6	+0700	10.25	Merged into Bacardi Corp 1986 @ $6.00.

NAME	DATE - PRICE	CURRENT PRICE	% GAIN LOSS	HIGH PRICE	NOTES
LSB INDUST(BB:LSBD)	9/85 - 2.25	1.25	- 0044	9.50	
LUNN IND(O:LUNN)	See Advanced Tech Products				
LVI GROUP(NI)	10/77 - 2.63	0.00	- 0100	8.63	Was Lehigh Valley. Ceased trading
LYNNWEAR CORP(OP)	3/79 - 2.75	0.00	- 0100	2.75	Bankrupt
MACANDREW/FOR(NYSE)	2/78 - 2.13	Priv @ 53.25	+2400	57.38	Went private early in '84 @ $53.25 per share.
MAGIC MARKER(OP)	9/81 - 0.31	0.00	- 0100	0.50	Bankrupt
MAGNETIC TECH(O:MTCC)	7/84 - 15.00	Merged @ 5.00	- 0073	6.50	1-for-10 rev 1/88. 3-for-1 2/94. Merged with SPS Tech.
MANATRON INC(O:MANA)	4/90 - 2.00	9.00	+0350	9.00	
MARCADE GROUP(NYSE)	See Aris Ind				
MARGO CARIBE(O:MRGO)	10/88 - 1.88	16.00	+0751	18.31	Was Margo Nursery
MARGO NURSERY(O:MRGO)	See Margo Caribe Inc				
MASSEY FERGUSON(NYSE)	See Varity Corp.				
MATEC CORP(A:MXC)	12/78 - 2.63	6.88	+0162	6.88	Was RSC Ind.
MAXCO INC(O:MAXC)	2/83 - 1.88	7.88	+0319	12.50	
MCRAE IND(A:MRI.A)	7/85 - 2.63	5.25	+0100	10.62	
MDC CORP(OTC)	See MDC Holdings.				
MDC HOLDINGS(N:MDC)	10/80 - 2.50	13.56	+0442	22.50	Was MDC Corp.
MEDALLION GP(ASE)	3/78 - 2.25	Merged @ 10.25	+0356	10.25	
MEDCOM INC(OTC)	11/78 - 2.38	Merged @ 35	+1371	35.00	
MEDIA PRODUCTS(NI)	1/88 - 2.44	0.00	-0100	3.50	Ceased trading
MEDICAL TECH(BB:MSYS)	7/89 - 8.76	0.56	-0094	11.25	Adjusted for 1-for-4 reverse split Jan '92.
MEGADATA CORP(BB:MDTA)	10/79 - 2.38	1.50	-0037	14.75	
MERIDIAN NATL(O:MRCO)	6/87 - 1.75	0.24	-0086	4.25	
MESA LABS(O:MLAB)	4/91 - 2.31	3.62	+0057	8.00	Was Mesa Medical.
MESA MED ICAL(OTC)	See Mesa Labs				
METALBANC CORP(OTC)	See Jillan's Entertainment.				
MHI GROUP(NYSE)	8/78 - 10.52	Tenderd @ 10.25	-0003	10.52	Restated 1-for-4 reverse split Nov '93. Was Mobile Home.
MHI GRP(NYSE)	3/89 - 4.52	Tenderd @ 10.25	+0126	10.52	Restated 1-for-4 reverse split Nov '93.
MICHIGAN GEN(NI)	10/81 - 3.00	0.00	-0100	14.00	Bankrupt
MICKELBERRY COMM(N)	3/91 - 2.50	Bought @ 4.25	+0070	4.25	Was Mickelberry Corp. Bought out by insider.
MICKELBERRY CORP(N)	See Mickelberry Comm				

NAME	DATE - PRICE	CURRENT PRICE	% GAIN LOSS	HIGH PRICE	NOTES
MICRO-INTEGRAT(BB:MINT)	11/97 - 2.94	0.75	-0074	4.00	
MICROFORM DATA(OTC)	See Amati Comm.				
MICROFRAME(O:MCFR)	See Ion Network				
MICROS SYS(O:MCRS)	10/84 - 1.25	52.88	+4130	60.56	2-for-1 split May '98
MICROS SYSTEM(O:MCRS)	11/81 - 1.13	52.88	+4580	54.00	2-for-1 split May '98
MICROS-T0-MAIN(O:MTMC)	2/95 - 3.53	7.62	+0116	7.63	
MICROSIZE INC(OP)	2/85 - 1.63	0.00	-0100	1.63	No Market
MIDLAND RESOUR(OTC)	See American Midland.				
MILLBROOK PRESS(O:MILB)	12/98 - 2.56	2.00	-0022	7.88	
MILLENIA INC(OP:MENA)	11/94 - 2.25	02.31	-0100	5.44	Was S.O.I. Industries; 1-for-8 rev 12/95, 1-for-100 rev 11/98.
MINING SER INT'L(O:MSIX)	5/90 - 2.44	2.50	+0002	19.00	
MISSOURI RSCH(OP)	See MRL Inc.				
MOBILE HOME(NYSE)	See MHI Group				
MONTEREY PASTA(O:PSTA)	9/98 - 1.13	3.62	+0220	4.63	
MOSCOM CORP(O:MSCM)	See Veramark Technologies				
MOTORVAC TECH(O:MVAC)	8/99 - 2.44	3.62	+0048	4.63	
MRL INC(OP)	10/78 - 1.75	0.00	-0100	3.13	No Market. Was Missouri Research.
MSR EXPLORATION(A:MSR)	7/80 - 1.63	16.38	+0598	16.38	Was MT States Res.
MT STATES RES(OTC)	See MSR Exploration				
NAT'L ENTER(OP)	See Empire Gold				
NAT'L ENVIRON CONTR(OP)	10/82 - 2.33	0.00	-0100	9.75	Restated for 4-for-3 split 6/83. No Market
NAT'L HEALTH ENH(O:NHES)	12/92 - 2.38	Acquired @ 11.31	+0375	14.00	Acquired by HBOC Inc @ 11.31
NAT'L HERITAGE(NYSE)	See Evergreen Health				
NAT'L HMO CORP(OTC)	See Nat'L Home Health				
NAT'L HOME HEALTH(O:NHHC)	2/90 - 2.00	4.06	+0103	7.75	Was Nat'l HMO Corp.
NAT'L HOME IND(NYSE)	See National Enterprises.				
NAT'L TECHTEAM(O:TEAM)	9/92 - 1.22	6.75	+0453	30.13	
NATHAN'S FAMOUS(OTC)	9/83 - 2.38	Merged @ 8.50	+0257	8.50	Merged Jun '87 with Equicor Group Ltd @ $8.50.
NEWMAN COMMUN(OTC)	See Index Inc.				
NOBILITY HOME(O:NOBH)	2/78 - 2.63	5.38	+0105	17.50	
NOODLE KADOODLE(O:NKID)	1/79 - 1.50	4.19	+0179	28.88	Was Greenman Bros. Adjusted 5-for-4 split Aug '86.

NAME	DATE - PRICE	CURRENT PRICE	% GAIN LOSS	HIGH PRICE	NOTES
NOVO CORP(NI)	9/84 - 2.75	0.00	-0100	3.75	Ceased trading
NUMEREX CORP(OTC)	1/89 - 3.00	Merged @ 4.25	+0042	4.25	
NY TEST LABS(NI)	12/83 - 1.38	0.00	-0100	4.00	Restated 2-for-1 split Aug '87. Ceased trading
OAK HILL SPORT(O:OHSC)	See Rexx Environmental Corp				
OAK IND(N:OAK)	6/88 - 6.25	Bought @ 75.00	+1100	80.50	Bought by Corning Inc @ 75.00 11/99. 1-for-5 reverse split 5/92.
OCEAN BIO-CHEM(O:OBCI)	07/93 - 3.25	1.75	-0046	3.50	
OILTECH(NI)	6/80 - 2.25	0.00	-0100	2.25	Bankrupt. Jan '84 1-for-10 reverse split.
OMNIAMERICA(O:XMIT)	2/96 - 2.25	Acquired @ 25.96	+1054	31.50	Was Specialty Telecon-structors. Acquired by Amer. Tower Corp. 2/99.
ON-SITE SOURCING(O:ONSS)	1/98 - 2.88	3.00	+0004	3.62	
ORANGE CO(N:OJ)	7/77 - 30.00	Merged @ 7.00	-0077	11.25	Merged with Reservoir Cap. 1-for-10 rev split 4/87. Was Amer. Agron.
ORMAND IND(NI)	6/79 - 2.88	0.00	-0100	9.38	Ceased trading
OSROW PROD(NI)	3/78 - 2.75	0.00	-0100	4.63	Ceased trading
OXFORD EXPLOR(OTC)	5/80 - 1.69	Merged @ .07	-0096	3.13	Merged Sep '85 forming Oxford Consolidated, Inc.
PAMEX FOODS(OTC)	See Pancho's Mexican Buffet				
PANCHO'S MEX BUF(O:PAMX)	10/80 - 6.75	3.59	-0047	15.88	Was Pamex Foods. 1-for-3 rev 1/99.
PASSPORT TRAVEL(OP)	11/82 - 2.25	0.00	-0100	2.88	No Market
PATRICK INDUS(O:PATK)	9/82 - 2.37	9.62	+0306	29.50	10% stock dividend paid Nov '88.
PATRICK INDUS(O:PATK)	5/78 - 2.59	9.62	+0271	29.50	10% stock dividend paid Nov '88.
PAY-O-MATIC(OTC)	11/79 - 2.13	Private @ 10	+0339	14.50	
PENTRON IND(ASE)	See Rotonics Mfg.				
PERLE SYSTEMS(O:PERL)	3/99 - 2.44	9.00	+0269	22.88	
PHOENIX FINAN(NI)	8/86 - 2.06	0.00	-0100	2.06	Became Raintree Financial in Oct '89.
PHOTO CONTROL(O:PHOC)	12/79 - 2.40	2.56	+0007	12.50	Restated 5-for-4 stock split Aug '93.
PHOTOCOMM(O:PCOM)	See Golden Genesis				
PIEDMONT IND(ASE)	6/78 - 1.75	0.00	-0100	2.63	Ceased trading
PIER 1 IMPT(N:PIR)	12/79 - 1.83	8.56	+0368	29.56	Restated 3-for-2 split Jul '86.

NAME	DATE - PRICE	CURRENT PRICE	% GAIN LOSS	HIGH PRICE	NOTES
PIONEER SYS(NI)	8/78 - 3.00	0.00	-0100	14.13	Ceased trading
PLASMA THERM(O:PTIS)	8/90 - 1.25	12.50	+0900	12.50	
PLAYERS INT'L(O:PLAY)	8/89 - 1.56	Bought @ 8.50	+0445	25.13	3-for-2 stock split. Bought by Harrah's Enter, @ 8.50 8/99.
POPULAR BANC(NI)	3/83 - 2.88	0.00	-0100	6.38	
PRAIRIE STATES(OTC)	5/81 - 0.50	0.00	-0100	0.66	Bankrupt
PRINCETON DIAG(ASE)	7/90 - 2.38	Merged @ 1.22	-0049	3.31	Merged with EDITEK(ASE) 2/94.
PRO-DEX INC(O:PDEX)	4/93 - 2.50	2.03	-0019	6.06	
PROF INVESTORS(NI)	5/81 - 2.13	0.00	-0100	10.75	Conservator appointed Dec '89 by OK Dept. of Ins.
PTI HOLDING(O:PTII)	6/95 - 2.38	1.22	-0049	10.63	
PUBCO CORP(O:PUBO)	5/87 - 13.80	8.75	-0037	11.62	Restated for 1-for-20 reverse split Aug '90.
PVC CONTAINER(O:PVCC)	4/85 - 1.06	4.56	+0330	9.75	
PYRAMID OIL(BB:PYOL)	5/79 - 2.25	0.81	-0064	13.88	
OUESTRONICS(OTC)	See Globestat Hldgs				
RAND INFO SYS(NI)	4/81 - 4.50	0.00	-0100	6.63	Restated 1-for-3 reverse split. Ceased trading
RAPIDATA(OTC)	9/77 - 3.00	Merged @ 16	+0433	16.75	
RCM TECHNOLOGIES(O:RCMT)	7/83 - 6.25	16.56	+0165	27.63	Adjusted for 1-for-5 reverse split 4/96
RECONDITIONED SYS(O:RESY)	5/99 - 2.75	2.50	-0009	3.88	
RECTISEL CORP(OTC)	3/84 - 3.00	Merged @ 5	+0067	5.00	
REDLAW INDUST(BB:RDLI)	1/85 - 2.25	0.03	-0099	5.88	
REGAL COMM(OP)	6/92 - 2.75	0.00	-0100	7.75	Bankrupt
RENT-A-WRECK AMER(O:RAWA)	12/94 - 1.13	2.00	-0077	2.66	
REXX ENVIRON CORP(A:REX)	6/81 - 5.50	9.00	+0064	12.63	1-for-2 rev 7/83. Was Oak Hill Sportswear
RICHMONT MINES(A:RIC)	10/98 - 2.56	1.50	-0041	3.25	
RIVER OAKS(NI)	7/88 - 0.63	0.00	-0100	1.00	Ceased trading
ROBERT HALMI(OTC)	4/81 - 2.74	Merged @ 1.90	-0030	10.00	Merged with Hal Roach into HRI Group Apr '88 @ 1.90/share.
ROBESON IND(OP)	8/82 - 2.38	0.00	-0100	6.88	Bankrupt
ROCKWELL DRILL(OTC)	8/81 - 1.69	Acquired @ .01	-0099	2.50	Acquired by Miramar Resources Feb '90, 20 Rockwell for 1 sh Miramar.
ROMTECH(O:ROMT)	See eGames Inc.				

NAME	DATE - PRICE	CURRENT PRICE	% GAIN LOSS	HIGH PRICE	NOTES
RONSON CORP(O:RONC)	5/80 - 6.75	2.31	+0066	7.25	Restated 1-for-3 reverse split Mar '88.
ROSS COSMETICS(OTC)	See Tristar Corp.				
ROTONICS MFG(A:RMI)	5/78 - 1.50	1.31	-0013	3.38	Was Pentron Ind, then Koala Technologies.
RPS PRODUCTS(NI)	11/78 - 1.88	0.00	-0100	3.50	Bankrupt
RSC INDUST(ASE)	See Matec Corporation.				
RUSCO IND(OP)	10/78 - 1.88	0.00	-0100	4.13	Bankrupt
S.O.I. INDUSTRIES(A:SOI)	See Millenia Inc				
SAHLEN & ASSOC(NI)	5/86 - 1.50	0.00	-0100	4.13	Bankrupt
SANDATA INC(O:SAND)	11/89 - 1.97	3.06	+0055	11.00	
SAV-A-STOP(NYSE)	7/77 - 2.75	Merged @ 16	+0482	17.13	
SCAT HOVERCRAFT(NI)	10/86 - 1.44	0.00	-0100	1.56	Ceased trading
SCHILLER(ASE)	1/78 - 2.25	Merged @ 13.50	+0500	13.50	
SCHOOL PICTURES(ASE)	3/82 - 3.00	Merged @ 11.50	+0283	11.50	Merged @ $11.50 Jul '88 with Jostens Inc.
SCIENCE ACCESS(OP)	2/87 - 12.00	Merged at .09	-0099	12.00	1-for-4 rev 11/93. Merged w. GTCO Corp. 12/95.
SCIENCE MGMT(OP)	11/79 - 2.88	Acquired @ 0.32	-0089	16.25	Acquired by Versar Inc Oct '97 @ 0.32
SCRIPTO INC(OTC)	1/81 - 2.19	Merged @ 2.44	+0011	4.00	
SEAPORT(NI)	12/77 - 0.81	0.00	-0100	3.88	Ceased trading
SECURITY ENV SYS(NI)	03/93 - 3.75	0.00	-0100	8.13	Restated for 1-for-3 reverse Jul '93.
SEMTECH CORP(O:SMTC)	6/86 - 0.53	66.25	+12400	77.88	2-for-1 split Jan '98. 2-for-1 split 10/99.
SENSORY SCIENCE(A:VCR)	12/97 - 2.38	3.12	+0031	4.94	Was Go-Video
SENTRY MFG(NI)	7/80 - 2.75	0.00	-0100	6.00	Ceased trading
SERVAMATIC SYS(NI)	6/83 - 2.31	0.00	-0100	3.13	Bankrupt
SHERWOOD BRANDS(A:SHD)	6/99 - 2.75	2.12	-0023	3.44	
SIGNATURE MOTORCARS(NI)	10/81 - 1.50	0.00	-0100	1.50	Was International Royalty & Oil. Ceased trading
SILVER STATE MN(OTC)	See U.S. Gold Corp.				
SMD INDUSTRIES(ASE)	7/79 - 2.63	Merged @ 8.50	+0223	12.25	Merged with American Greetings Dec '86 @ $8.50.
SMITHFIELD FD(A:SFD)	7/77 - 0.29	16.19	+5483	39.00	2-for-1 split 10/86 2-for-1 9/88, 2-for-1 1/98.
SOFTNET SYSTEMS(O:SOFN)	7/78 - 20.00	37.25	-0007	40.25	1-for-8 reverse Nov '98. Was Vader Group
SONOMAWEST HLDGS(O:SWHI)	7/81 - 2.88	5.25	+0082	14.00	Was Vacu - Dry

NAME	DATE - PRICE	CURRENT PRICE	% GAIN LOSS	HIGH PRICE	NOTES
SOUTHERN HOSP(NI)	11/80 - 2.38	0.00	-0100	7.50	Ceased trading
SPARTAN MOTOR(O:SPAR)	12/86 - 1.33	4.00	+0201	34.75	3-for-2 split 9/92 3-for-2 split 6/94.
SPEC TELECONSTRU(O:SCTR)	See Omni America				
SPECTRAN CORP(O:SPTR)	12/90 - 2.56	Acquired @ 9.00	+0252	23.50	Acquired by Lucent Technologies @ 9.00
SPORTSMAN GUIDE(O:SGDE)	4/87 - 2.63	3.25	+0024	8.00	
STANDARD LOGIC(NI)	See Appoint Technologies				
STAODYN(O:SDYN)	12/85 - 2.00	Merged @ 3.32	+0066	11.25	Merged with Rehabilicare Inc @ 3.32; Was Staodynamics.
STAODYNAMICS(OTC)	See Staodyn				
STAR CLASSICS(OP)	See Data Trend Systems.				
STERLING ELEC(A:SEC)	4/84 - 2.75	Merged @ 21.00	+0664	21.00	Merged with Marshall Ind Jan '98 @ 21.00
STERLING ELECT(A:SEC)	9/77 - 1.00	Merged @ 21.00	+2000	21.00	Merged with Marshall Ind Jan '98 @ 21.00
STERLING EXTRU(ASE)	1/81 - 2.50	Merged @ 23.50	+0840	23.50	Acquired by Baker Perkins @ $23.50 @ share.
STERLING O/OK(NI)	2/81 - 1.81	0.00	-0100	2.00	Ceased trading
STERNER LIGHT(OTC)	1/81 - 2.25	Merged @ 17	+0656	18.38	Acquired by Churchill Companies Jul '89 @ $17.00.
SUN COAST IND(N:SN)	3/86 - 12.50	Buyout @ 10.75	-0014	17.00	1-for-5 rev Jan '92 Was Sun Coast Plastics. Acqed by Kerr Grp Mar '98
SUN COAST PLAS(OTC)	See SunCoast Industries				
SUNERGY COMMUN(OTC)	9/82 - 2.06	Merged @ 0.50	-0075	7.88	Merged with River Oaks Industries @ $0.50 @ share.
SYNERGY BRANDS(O:SYBR)	5/96 - 29.75	3.47	-0088	5.13	1-for-25 rev 5/97. Was Krantor Corp.
TAX CORP AMER(OTC)	9/79 - 1.88	0.00	-0100	1.88	Bankrupt
TCC INDUSTRIES(OP:TELE)	6/87 - 2.38	0.06	-0083	10.12	Was Telecom Corp.
TECH-SYM CORP(N:TSY)	5/78 - 2.75	17.75	+0545	35.00	
TECHNODYNE(NI)	9/87 - 2.63	0.00	-0100	2.88	Ceased trading
TEL'PH SPEC(NI)	3/84 - 1.88	0.00	-0100	2.38	Bankrupt
TELECOM CORP(NYSE)	See TCC Ind				
TELETEK(OP)	12/95 - 1.28	0.00	-0100	9.38	No Market
TELEVISION TECH(NI)	3/85 - 0.78	0.00	-0100	1.75	
TELEX CORP(NYSE)	6/77 - 2.50	Merged @ 62	+2380	62.00	Merged Jan '88 with Memorex Int'l @ $62.00.

NAME	DATE - PRICE	CURRENT PRICE	% GAIN LOSS	HIGH PRICE	NOTES
TENNA CORP(NI)	6/78 - 2.63	0.00	-0100	3.75	Ceased trading
TENSOR CORP(ASE)	See VaderGroup.				
TFI COMPANIES(ASE)	See Cardiff Equities.				
THERAGENICS CORP(N:TGX)	6/91 - 1.31	12.00	+0816	57.25	2-for-1 split Apr '98
THERMWOOD CORP(A:THM)	11/95 - 10.00	6.50	-0035	14.37	Adjusted for 1-for-5 reverse Jan '98
THOR ENERGY(NI)	2/84 - 5.25	0.00	-0100	3.50	Adjusted for 3-for-2 split '92. Ceased trading
THREE-FIVE SYS(N:TFS)	5/91 - 0.99	45.31	+4477	55.75	2-for-1 split 5/94, 4-for-3 split 12/99.
THT INC(O:TXHI)	05/93 - 2.94	Private @ 3.75	+0028	3.75	Went private @ 3.75 3/99
TIDEL TECH(O:ATMS)	2/99 - 2.44	4.56	+0087	4.94	
TIDWELL IND(ASE)	8/77 - 2.88	0.00	-0100	20.63	Bankrupt
TIVOLI IND(O:TVLI)	10/96 - 1.00	Acquired @ 4.50	+0350	4.50	Acquired by Targetti Sankey @ 4.50 11/99
TJT INC(O:AXLE)	5/97 - 1.81	0.69	-0062	2.43	
TM CENTURY(BB:TMCI)	8/87 - 2.88	0.72	-0075	3.78	Was TM Coninunications.
TM CENTURY(BB:TMCI)	11/93 - 3.13	0.72	-0077	3.78	
TM COMMUNICATION(OTC)	See TM Century				
TNR TECHNICAL(BB:TNRK)	4/86 - 18.00	7.50	-0058	6.75	1-for-200 reverse Feb '92
TOTH ALUMINUM(OP)	7/83 - 2.00	0.00	-0100	4.25	No Market
TRANSACT INT(O:TACT)	12/82 - 2.50	7.00	+0180	14.63	
TRANSMATION(O:TRNS)	8/84 - 1.32	2.78	+0111	10.75	Adjusted for 2-for-1 split Jul '97.
TRANSMEDIA NETWK(N:TMN)	6/90 - 0.63	5.00	+0710	20.75	3-for-2 split 10/93 3-for-2 split 4/92.
TRANSNET CORP(BB:TRNT)	6/82 - 2.75	1.97	-0028	4.13	In process of being acquired by G.E. Capital Inc.
TRI-SOUTH IN(NYSE)	See Avalon Corporation.				
TRINITY BIOTECH(O:TRIBY)	10/97 - 2.72	4.50	+0065	4.50	
TRISTAR CORP(O:TSAR)	6/85 - 1.36	6.00	+0341	44.50	2-for-1 2/92. Was Ross Cosmetics.
TVI CORP(BB:TVIN)	2/84 - 1.81	0.11	-0094	2.13	Was TVI Energy.
TVI ENERGY(OTC)	See TVI Corporation.				
TWENTY-FIRST CENT(OTC)	See Cannon Pictures				
U.S. GOLD(BB:USGL)	4/85 - 1.16	0.29	-0075	3.63	Was Silver State Min.
UDS INC(OTC)	7/78 - 2.75	Merged @ .25	-0091	3.25	Merged with Artex Investors Inc. Feb '85 @ $0.25.

✦ MAKING DOLLARS WITH PENNIES ✦

NAME	DATE - PRICE	CURRENT PRICE	% GAIN LOSS	HIGH PRICE	NOTES
UMET PROPERTY(NYSE)	See Hallwood Group.				Shares converted to Hallwood Grp thru series of stock transactions.
UNICO INC(BB:UICO)	5/88 - 35.28	Bought @ .10	-0097	2.94	Was CMS Advertising. 1-for-4 rev. 12/97.,Bot by Next Generation 1/99
UNITED ED/SOFT(NI)	11/85 - 1.83	0.00	-0100	16.38	Restated 3-for-2 stock split Apr '88, ceased trading.
UNITED FOODS(A:UFD.A)	8/80 - 0.94	Buyout @ 3.50	+0272	4.38	2-for-1 split in '83. Buyout by management @ 3.50 5/99.
UNIVER AMER FINAN(O:UHCO)	9/94 - 2.63	4.31	+0064	4.94	Was Universal Holding Corp
UNIVERSAL HOLDING(O:UHCO)	See Universal AmerFinan				
UNIVERSAL PHON(NI)	4/80 - 3.00	0.00	-0100	10.25	Ceased trading
UTAH MEDICAL(N:UM)	12/86 - 1.33	6.94	+0422	24.75	1-for-10 rev split 12/91 3-for-2 3/93.
VACU-DRY CO(O:VDRY)	See Sonoma West Hldgs				
VADER GROUP(NI)	See Softnet Systems				
VALHI INC(N:VHI)	1/86 - 2.25	11.06	+0392	18.25	Was LLC Corp.
VARITY CORP(N:VAT)	7/86 - 25.00	Merged @ 51.96	+0108	51.96	1-for-10 rev 8/91. Merged with Lucas Corp.
VELO BIND(OTC)	11/77 - 10.00	Merged @ 9.77	-0002	15.50	Bought out by General Binding Corp Nov '91 for $9.77/share.
VENDO CO(NYSE)	9/81 - 2.88	Merged @ 9	+0213	16.25	Merged May '88 with Sanden Corp @ $9.00.
VERAMARK TECH(O:VERA)	10/87 - 2.75	8.50	+0230	14.75	Was Moscom Corp
VERIT IND(NI)	11/80 - 2.25	0.00	-0100	20.00	Ceased trading
VIATECH INC(ASE)	See Continental Can				
VIDEOLABS INC(O:VLAB)	4/96 - 2.50	4.47	+0079	4.47	
VISUAL ELECT(OTC)	See Visual Industries.				
VISUAL IND(NI)	7/85 - 2.19	0.00	-0100	4.88	Ceased trading. Was Visual Electronics.
VITRONICS CORP(A:VTC)	4/88 - 2.50	Merged @ 1.90	-0024	3.38	Merged with DTI Intermediate @ 1.90
VOLUME MERCH(ASE)	1/79 - 2.38	Merged @ 7.50	+0215	10.25	
WARRANTECH(BB:PS)	10/92 - 2.38	1.30	-0045	15.38	
WAXMAN IND(BB:WAXX)	1/80 - 0.44	0.43	-0002	17.00	3-for-2 split 4/85 2-for-1 split 12/86 3-for-2 7/88.
WCM CAPITAL INC(O:WCMC)	5/88 - 7.68	6.00	-0022	6.00	Was Franklin Cons. 1-for-3 split 12/99.

✦ HISTORICAL REVIEW ✦

NAME	DATE - PRICE	CURRENT PRICE	% GAIN LOSS	HIGH PRICE	NOTES
WELLS AMERICAN(NI)	10/87 - 2.75	0.00	-0100	3.75	Ceased trading
WINDLAND ELECT(A:WEX)	7/98 - 2.63	2.69	+0002	3.63	Switched to the AMEX on Jan '00.
WORLCO INC(OP)	6/81 - 1.44	0.00	-0100	2.50	No Market
WINMILL & CO(O:WNMLA)	11/83 - 10.16	2.00	-0080	16.00	1-for-5 rev 12/85. Was Bull & Bear Group.
ZEGARELLI GRP INT(OP)	3/97 - 1.75	0.00	-0100	2.03	Was Cosmetic Group Int'l. Ceased trading.
ZYTEC COMPUTER(OTC)	See Zytec Systems.				
ZYTEC SYSTEMS(OP)	2/87 - 1.25	0.00	-0100	2.13	Ceased trading. Was Zytec Computer.

ABOUT THE AUTHOR

Born in Celina, Ohio, Bowser exhibited an early interest in journalism. He was editor of his high school newspaper for three years.

After high school, he worked on weekly Ohio newspapers, first in Coldwater and then in Eaton. On the Eaton Press-Review he was the editor and a "string" correspondent for the Associated Press, the *Dayton Journal Herald* and the *Cincinnati Times-Star*.

His newspaper career was interrupted by World War II. During a tour in the Air Force, he went from a headquarters clerk to an intelligence officer in the Philippines.

After World War II he was employed on newspapers in California: Monrovia, Arcadia and in the San Fernando Valley. But, again the Air Force called. This time it was the Korean "conflict." During those hostilities he spent most of his time in Taegu, Korea.

But, by then he decided to make a career of the Air Force. He served a total of 24 years. Besides the Philippines, Japan and Korea, he was stationed in Germany, Turkey and Vietnam, plus various state-side bases. He retired in April 1970 with the rank of lieutenant colonel.

While at his last duty station in the Air Force—Langley Air Force Base in Hampton, Virginia—Bowser became interested in the stock market. And, he decided to make the stock market his speciality during his post-military career.

His first step in that new career was to go to college to broaden his business background. In the spring of 1973 he graduated *magna cum laude* from Thomas Nelson Community College in Hampton, Virginia, with two associate degrees—one in accounting and the other in business administration.

From 1973 to 1979 he further studied the stock market, refining his techniques for investing in low-priced equities. It was also during this period he decided to concentrate on stocks selling for $3 a share or less. Too, he then determined the format for the newsletter, principally by mailing it to a select group across the country and considering their various suggestions.

Although it initially only had 40 paid subscribers in 1979, *The Bowser Report* is now in the top 5% in circulation among the hundreds of investment newsletters.

Bowser finds his experience as a military intelligence analyst is not dissimilar to his present role as a securities analyst. The technique is the same—bringing together various facets of information and from this mass of information, deducing future action. Also, his many years of writing simplifies his task of monthly preparing *The Bowser Report*.

INDEX

Those who say the "little guy" doesn't have a chance against the big institutions have it wrong. One of the best things in the small investor's favor, in fact, is the very incompetence of most large investors.

More often than not, the great institutions—the banks, insurance companies, pension funds and mutual funds—are prey to precisely the faults they condescendingly, and incorrectly, ascribe to small investors.

The institutions tend to act with emotion rather than sense, to panic and stampede, to buy or sell when the rest of the crowd is doing exactly the same thing, even to buy or sell exactly the same stocks. Thinking for oneself is such a rarity in that overheated climate that it can—and often does—put the "little guy" way ahead at the eventual finish line.

— LOUIS RUKEYSER

The Bowser Report

THE PREMIER NEWSLETTER FOR MINIPRICED STOCKS SINCE 1976

If you enjoyed reading this book and the concept outlined, you will also enjoy reading *The Bowser Report*. Highlights of this 10-page monthly newsletter are:

(1) *Company of the Month* – One stock is selected for detailed analysis.

(2) *Minipriced Stocks in Buying Range* – A list of those stocks on the NYSE, ASE and OTC markets that have a Bowser Rating of 8 or more.

(3) *Follow-Through* – Past recommendations are continuously reviewed.

(4) *Feature Articles* – Feature articles are written in an informal, humorous style.

(5) *Subscriber's Forum* – In which we respond to letters from our subscribers on issues of universal interest.

ALL THIS IS AVAILABLE FOR ONE OF THE
LOWEST SUBSCRIPTION PRICES AROUND!

For a sample copy of this unique newsletter, just mail in this coupon.

- — — — — — — — — — — — — — — — — — — —

R. Max Bowser
The Bowser Report
P.O. Box 6278
Newport News, VA 23606

Please send to me FREE and without obligation a sample copy of *The Bowser Report*.

Name _____

Address _____

City _____ State _____ Zip _____

P.O. BOX 6278   NEWPORT NEWS, VIRGINIA 23606   (757) 877-5979

MILLIONAIRE RESOURCE LIST

The following books and audiocassettes are informative and based on tried and proven methods by the authors. You may request these products from your book dealer, or order directly from the publisher.

AUDIOCASSETTES

How To Get Rich and Stay Rich
A Live Speech by Fred J. Young   **Retail Price: $9.95**

This popular and humorous speech by Fred J. Young explains how this multimillionaire made his fortune by investing a portion of his salary in a few shares of stock on a regular basis. At this time, his net worth is over $3 million.

Don't Get Mad — Get Rich
A Live Speech by Fred J. Young   **Retail Price: $9.95**

Humorous true adventures that Fred J. Young had during his journey toward becoming a multimillionaire. Fun to listen to and full of stock market wisdom.

BOOKS

Making Dollars With Pennies:
How the Small Investor Can Beat the Wizards on Wall Street
Author: R. Max Bowser   **Retail Price: $19.95**

Penny Stock Winners:
True Stories of Successful Investors
Author: R. Max Bowser   **Retail Price: $19.95**

A collection of interviews of fifteen successful penny stock investors. They share their investment secrets.

All the above audiocassettes and books are published by:

MARATHON INTERNATIONAL BOOK COMPANY
P.O. Box 40   Phone: (812) 273-4672
Madison, IN 47250-0040   Fax: (812) 273-4672
U.S.A.   e-mail: books@marathonbooks.net
                               Web Site: www.marathonbooks.net

---

Contact us for a free catalog of
hard-to-find stock market books and cassette tapes.

ORDER FORM

Quantity		Unit Price	Total For Product
	AUDIOCASSETTES		
_____	*How To Get Rich and Stay Rich* A speech by Fred J. Young	$9.95	$_____
_____	*Don't Get Mad — Get Rich* A speech by Fred J. Young	$9.95	$_____
	BOOKS		
_____	*Making Dollars With Pennies: How The Small Investor Can Beat The Wizards On Wall Street* Book by R. Max Bowser	$19.95	$_____
_____	*Penny Stock Winners: True Stories of Successful Investors* Book by R. Max Bowser	$19.95	$_____

POSTAGE

Regular Mail: $2 for first book or audiocassette, $1 for each additional.
Priority Mail: $4 for first book or audiocassette, $1 for each additional.
Foreign Orders (Air Mail): $4 for first book or audiocassette, $2 for each additional.

Total Amount for Products Ordered: $_____

Total Amount for Shipping: $_____

Grand Total Amount: $_____

Name _____

Address _____

City _____ State _____ Zip _____

Send order form and payment in U.S. funds to:

MARATHON INTERNATIONAL BOOK COMPANY
P.O. Box 40
Madison, IN 47250-0040
U.S.A.

ORDER FORM

Quantity		Unit Price	Total For Product
	AUDIOCASSETTES		
_____	*How To Get Rich and Stay Rich* A speech by Fred J. Young	$9.95	$_____
_____	*Don't Get Mad — Get Rich* A speech by Fred J. Young	$9.95	$_____
	BOOKS		
_____	*Making Dollars With Pennies: How The Small Investor Can Beat The Wizards On Wall Street* Book by R. Max Bowser	$19.95	$_____
_____	*Penny Stock Winners: True Stories of Successful Investors* Book by R. Max Bowser	$19.95	$_____

POSTAGE

Regular Mail: $2 for first book or audiocassette, $1 for each additional.
Priority Mail: $4 for first book or audiocassette, $1 for each additional.
Foreign Orders (Air Mail): $4 for first book or audiocassette, $2 for each additional.

Total Amount for Products Ordered: $_____

Total Amount for Shipping: $_____

Grand Total Amount: $_____

Name _____

Address _____

City _____ State _____ Zip _____

Send order form and payment in U.S. funds to:

MARATHON INTERNATIONAL BOOK COMPANY
P.O. Box 40
Madison, IN 47250-0040
U.S.A.

R. Max Bowser